David took up writing late ... ... as a Chartered Architect mainly in London and won four design awards. After retiring from architecture, he became the Editor of a monthly golf publication entitled *The Gold Club Secretary* for nine years. It was during this period that his writing became more than a hobby. This is the seventh book he has written. His sixth book, *England's Finest Links,* was shortlisted for the sports book of the year in 2012; it came third in its class.

To my wife, Lesley, who has had to put up with me being glued to the computer for far too long.

David L Dobby

THE CONDUIT

AUSTIN MACAULEY PUBLISHERS
LONDON * CAMBRIDGE * NEW YORK * SHARJAH

Copyright © David L Dobby 2025

The right of David L Dobby to be identified as the author of this work has been asserted by the author in accordance with sections 77 and 78 of the Copyright, Designs and Patents Act 1988.

All rights reserved. No part of this publication may be reproduced, stored in a retrieval system, or transmitted in any form or by any means, electronic, mechanical, photocopying, recording, or otherwise, without the prior permission of the publishers.

Any person who commits any unauthorised act in relation to this publication may be liable to criminal prosecution and civil claims for damages.

The story, the experiences, and the words are the author's alone.

A CIP catalogue record for this title is available from the British Library.

ISBN 9781035884902 (Paperback)
ISBN 9781035884919 (ePub e-book)

www.austinmacauley.com

First Published 2025
Austin Macauley Publishers Ltd®
1 Canada Square
Canary Wharf
London
E14 5AA

Table of Contents

Preview	9
Chapter One: The Background	11
Chapter Two: Early Freemasonry	17
Chapter Three: Early Golf Clubs and Societies	36
Chapter Four: Early Military Field Lodges	74
Chapter Five: Social Strata in the Late 18th and 19th Century	79
Chapter Six: Early Golf Clubs and Societies and Their Association with Freemasonry	93
Chapter Seven: The Growth of Freemasonry	119
Chapter Eight: The Influence of the Military During the 18th and 19th Centuries	130
Chapter Nine: The Spread of Freemasonry Around the World	144
Chapter Ten: The Spread of Golf Around the World	152
Chapter Eleven: The Military Connection The Conduit	163
Chapter Twelve: Summary	171
Appendices	173

Appendix One Earliest Golf Clubs in UK   *175*

Appendix Two Earliest Overseas Golf Clubs   *181*

Appendix Three Military Field Lodges Prior to 1860   *183*

Appendix Four List of Regiments with Masonic Lodges   *188*

Appendix Five Overseas Posting of
Regiments with Military Lodges Prior to 1860   *198*

Appendix Six Extracts from a Talk Given by W Bro R M
Lacey Entitled Masonic Heroes   *206*

Appendix Seven Research Material   *209*

Preview

When I started this research to establish a link between Freemasonry and the foundation of golf clubs, I had no idea where it would lead me. The research has taken me through the history of both Freemasonry and golf clubs and golf societies, plus the history of the military, which surprisingly became the important link to this research and to the spread of both around the UK and the world.

Much has already been established on these three subjects, and I make no apology for using the text of published works on these histories; to paraphrase them would not do justice to the original authors and due credit has been given to the authors and their publications in all instances.

I have also been fortunate to be supplied with original material from some of the golf clubs featured in this research and I thank them for their assistance. I made initial enquiries of 39 golf clubs and golf societies. 22 responded of which 16 had some positive results. Where there was found to be a gap in my research of these clubs, some of the details have been obtained from their own websites.

In addition, I give my thanks to Angela Howe, Museum and Heritage Director, British Golf Museum, for providing me with background information on the formation of the Royal & Ancient Golf Club of St Andrews.

Sadly, much of the early history of Scottish golf clubs and golf societies is no longer available, either being lost by decay, fire, or destruction, which is a pity, as this early era has great significance to the history of both the golf club and Freemasonry. Likewise, the detailed history of early Scottish lodges was also limited and closely guarded. Whereas the history of early regiments is well documented.

I have, therefore, tried to piece together the relationship of those who played golf in those early years to Freemasonry, many of whom were officers in the militia, and hope that, despite the limited information available, I have succeeded in establishing that link.

Chapter One
The Background

In the year 1534, parliament declared Henry VIII the Supreme Head of the English Church. The monasteries were sacked in 1538 and Henry's Act disendowing the religious fraternities was passed in 1547. These were troubling times until Elizabeth took over.

However, the political merging of England and Scotland was still unresolved and became a looming question on the death of Elizabeth I, in 1603. She died unmarried and childless, consequently the crown passed to her cousin, 37-year-old James VI of Scotland, despite being the son of Mary Queen of Scots, who was executed by Elizabeth in 1587.

The new Scottish king accepted the transition without prejudice, occupying the thrones of Scotland and England plus Ireland in what became known as the 'Union of Crowns'.

James moved his court to London, ordered the creation of the Union Jack, and only returned to Scotland once during his lifetime. He tried to persuade the two parliaments to merge, but the idea was not entertained by either nation.

Delegations of Scottish and English MPs met several times during the turbulent 17th century to discuss a possible union, but no treaty materialised. Only in the 1690s, did attitudes change.

Scotland was nearly bankrupt and in a desperate bid to restore its finances, some 2,500 Scottish pioneers set off to found a colony in what is now Panama, but they were hopelessly ill-equipped and thwarted by disease. Only a few hundred of the settlers survived.

The 'Darien Scheme', as it was called, lost £233,000, which was about 25% of the nation's capital, a sum that was invested by thousands of families. Consequently, many of the Scottish elite began to see a union with England and access to its established trade routes as the only route to survival.

During the middle of the 17th century, England was plagued with civil war brought about by a loss of faith in the ability of the government under Charles I to effectively govern.

The English civil war was fought between the Parliamentarians (Roundheads) and the Royalists (Cavaliers) in three armed conflicts between the years 1642–1646, 1648–1649 and 1649–1651.

The Parliamentarians finally won at the Battle of Worcester on 3rd September 1651, which resulted in the trial and execution of Charles I, the exile of his son Charles II and the replacement of the English monarchy with a republic under Oliver Cromwell.

Constitutionally, the wars established the precedent that an English monarch cannot govern without parliament's consent. The concept of parliament being the ruling power of England was, however, only established in 1688, as part of the Glorious Revolution.

The Glorious Revolution of 1688–1689, replaced the reigning King James II, with the joint monarchy of his protestant daughter Mary and her Dutch husband, William of Orange. This was the keystone of the Whig (those opposed to a Catholic succession) history of Britain.

King William and Queen Mary were keen to unite the two countries to simplify the succession of their heirs, but England's ruling elite didn't see the point. Scottish commissioners, who were sent south to negotiate, faced disinterest from Westminster, as did another proposal for union in 1695.

It was only in 1700, when the next heir to the crowns of England and Scotland died at the age of 11, namely William, the Duke of Gloucester, that the fate of Scotland became an urgent priority.

In 1702, William of Orange died eight years after his wife and was succeeded by his sister-in-law, Queen Anne, who was the younger daughter of James II. 12 years later, George I succeeded Queen Anne in 1714, he was the grandson of Elizabeth Stuart and Frederick V, Count Palatine of the Rhine.

George I died in 1727 and the throne passed to his son, George II, who reigned until 1760. These were turbulent years for the monarchy.

The Scottish parliament, spurned by the arrogant English, passed the 'Act of Security' in 1704 enabling them to choose their own monarch. The Act threatened to tear up the 'Union of Crowns' and reactivate its historic alliance with France, with whom England was then at war.

England immediately reacted and on 6 December 1704, introduced two Bills in the Lords. The first offered Scotland fresh negotiations towards a full Union, a single parliament and free trade. The second, known as the 'Aliens Bill', threatened a ban on Scottish imports, of which 50% went to England unless Scotland agreed to the Hanoverian succession.

The showdown drove national feelings to new heights. However, the Duke of Hamilton, until then the chief opponent to a Union, decided the country had no choice.

"Our independency is now a jest," he said.

The final votes on the 25 articles were conducted in an atmosphere of furious horse-trading, corruption and street protest in 1706. It was not until a sum of £398,085 was given to Scotland as part of the negotiations to cover the huge debts arising from the Darien Scheme, that the 'Treaty of Union' was enabled.

Sadly, £20,000 of this sum was given out in bribes and the lenders of the debt were never paid in full.

Robert Burns wrote, *We are bought and sold for English gold. Such a parcel of rogues in a nation.*

The Union led to riots across Scotland and Martial Law was declared. Sir John Clerk of Penicuik, who negotiated for the Union, admitted it was *contrary to the inclinations of at least three-fourths of the Kingdom.*

Some 96 petitions were presented in 1706, showing deep discontent that later burst out in the 'Jacobite uprisings' of 1715 and 1745. The aim of these uprisings was to reinstall Scotland's lost Stuart kings, who were descendants of James VI.

For the 60 years following William III's accession to the throne in 1688, the exiled Stuarts clung tenaciously to their dream of regaining the kingdom they had lost. The deposed

James II died in 1701, to be succeeded by his son James III, the so-called 'Old Pretender'.

He in turn was succeeded as claimant by his son, the 'Young Pretender', Charles Edward 'Bonnie Prince Charlie'. Under these three monarchs-in-exile, Jacobite circles on the continent of Europe were to remain hotbeds of conspiracy and political intrigue. Only after the invasion and full-scale military operations of 1745–46, was this threat at last to recede.

The bloody defeat of 'Bonnie Prince Charlie', James's great-great grandson, at Culloden in 1745, led to the final dismantling of the old clan systems in the Scottish Highlands and the last vestiges of ancient self-government.

William and Mary, and Anne were popular monarchs. However, there were many who inveighed against the detested German sovereigns and agitated for a return of the Stuarts, whom they regarded as the country's rightful dynasty.

Michael Baigent & Richard Leigh in their book 'The Temple and the Lodge' claim, *The fissures of British society were to be reflected in Freemasonry.* They record that after the French Revolution in 1688, Freemasonry continued to survive and the number of lodges significantly grew.

It is thought that whilst many of the earlier lodges were pro-Stuart or Tory, they did not contribute to Jacobite espionage, conspiracy or propaganda, despite being closely linked with the Stuarts. Freemasons lodges during the early part of the 18th century, were either Whig or Tory, Hanoverian or Jacobite.

The split was conceived as the Tories in England and the Jacobites abroad and it was these two who established the future of Freemasonry based on their historical foundations.

All other developments in the Craft became branches from these two mainstreams.

There were in England some notable freemasons who were professed Jacobites, i.e., the Duke of Wharton and, following the suppression of the Jacobites in 1745, several eminent freemasons were sentenced to death for their support of the rebellion.

Others escaped to France and became influential in the dissemination of Freemasonry throughout Europe. Notably, the Duke of Wharton, who became the Grand Master of Freemasonry in France.

Thus, the scene is set for the consolidation of the Union and the development of Freemasonry from being initially operative to speculative.

Chapter Two
Early Freemasonry

It was during this period of unrest, followed by consolidation that both Freemasonry and the game of golf began to flourish. Freemasonry is recorded for the first time in 1646 with the making of Elias Ashmole a freemason at Warrington.

Thus, it may be perceived that the bridge between the disendowment of the religious guilds by Henry VIII and the making of Ashmole a freemason is but one century.

Bernard Jones in his publication 'The Freemasons' Guide and Compendium' states:

It is conjectured by some that during those 99 years one or two cells, or lodges, of a particular mystery, kept themselves alive through those four generations and that as a consequence we have in Freemasonry the only surviving medieval Craft esotery.

The old Scots operatives are well-known to have had their secret mode of recognition and their mason word. There are weighty authorities that believe English Freemasonry did, in fact, derive a great deal from the Scottish system, but it is difficult to see that Scotland had any masonic system, which by itself could have developed into the symbolic Craft known to freemasons of the early 1700s.

The fact that a speculative lodge was known to have existed in England in 1646, implies that there must have been other lodges operating at that time. Much is known about Scottish operative lodges during this period, which had speculative members as well as practical craftsmen but there are few details recorded of the early English lodges.

There is, however, the 'Regius Manuscript' that contains the medieval poem frequently used in early masonic ritual (believed by Halliwell to have been written in 1390) that was found in the library of John Theyer, a royalist lawyer who served in the king's army.

Charles II (1630–1685), purchased Theyer's library on his death and King George III, later presented it to the British Museum in 1757.

The early existence of lodges pre–1717 is confirmed by a record of Sir George Tempest presiding over a lodge in York 1705–06. This was a lodge that included many influential men. In 1717 the lodge also met in Bradford where it is recorded that 18 gentlemen were admitted.

Not all lodges advanced to speculative lodges, some, such as Alnwick Lodge in Northumberland, were initially wholly operative and did not become speculative until 1779. Prior to 1717, there were lodges recorded in Warrington, Chester, York, Chichester and London.

Jones further recaps:

- *In 1621 and 1631, there were acceptations into the London Company of Freemasons.*
- *In the 1640–50 period, on a scrap of paper written by Randle Holme, who was a mason, are words referring to the words and signs of a freemason.*
- *In 1646, Elias Ashmole was made a mason at Warrington.*
- *In 1648, a Warden of the London Company paid one pound for coming on the acceptation.*
- *In a list written around 1673, Randle Holme gives the names of 27 persons relating to the lodge at Chester.*
- *In 1676, a published advertisement mentions the Company of Accepted Masons.*
- *In 1682, Elias Ashmole attended a Lodge of Masons, among those present being many members of the company.*
- *In 1686, Dr Robert Pope printed many references to the Society of Freemasons, and in that same year, John Aubrey referred to the fraternity of Adopted Masons or Freemasons.*
- *In 1688, Randle Holme spoke of the antiquity of the fellowship of masons.*
- *In 1691, Aubrey recorded the adoption of Sir Christopher Wren and others as brethren of the Fraternity of Accepted Masons.*
- *In 1693, the York No. 4 MS. gave the names of the Lodge.*
- *In 1695/96, Edward Hall was made a mason at Chichester.*

> - *In 1709 and 1710, the Tatler referred to free Masons and a pamphlet dated 1710, that mentioned a certain company called the Free Masons.*

There are at least 20 Scottish operative lodges recorded prior to 1700 but none of these were known to have any symbolic working. In 1736, when Scotland's Grand Lodge was founded, invitations to join were sent to approximately 100 lodges and a response was received from 33. Nine out of the 20 pre–1700 lodges became founder members of the Scottish Grand Lodge, see listed below:

- Edinburgh (Mary's Chapel) No. 1
- Aberdeen
- Dundee
- Aitcheson's Haven (Extinct)
- Kilwinning (known as Lodge Mother Kilwinning No. 0).
- Dunfermline (No. 26)
- Canongate Kilwinning, No. 2, which has and still uses the oldest lodge room in the world
- Old Inverness Kilwinning, now known as Old Kilwinning St John
- Hamilton, now known as Hamilton Kilwinning

Bernard Jones further records that as far back as the Reformation certain Scots lodges welcomed aristocratic gentlemen as honorary members. In 1600, Mary's Chapel Lodge admitted John Boswell as an honorary member and in 1641 the same lodge admitted the Rt. Hon. Mr Robert Moray

(Murray), who was the General Quartermaster to the Army of Scotland.

These early lodges give us a clear insight into the strength of Freemasonry in Scotland prior to the formation of their Grand Lodge in 1736. It also establishes that the ritual was practised by the more affluent members of society, many of whom were also officers in the military.

At that time these honourable gentlemen were frequently called upon to defend their country whenever and wherever the occasion arose.

David Stevenson in his book 'Origins of Freemasonry' brings further light to this subject highlighting the impact that William Schaw had on the development of Freemasonry.

Schaw was the Master of Works for Scotland, i.e. the architect/project manager of all the King's buildings, and laid down the first and second statutes that formed the basis of Freemasonry, as we know it today. The two statutes were dated 28 December 1598 and 28 December 1599, respectively.

Schaw died in 1602 but before his death, he produced a third document that became the first St Clair (of Roslyn) Charter. Schaw intended to gain King James VI's approval for the privileges of masons, but it was never obtained.

He, therefore, agreed that William St Clair and his heirs should obtain from the king jurisdiction over masons as hereditary patrons, thereby protecting the masonic Craft. There were seven lodges represented by the Charter, namely: Aitchison's Haven, Dunfermline, Edinburgh, Haddington, Kilwinning, St Andrews and Stirling.

In 1628, a second St Clair Charter was produced with the approval of six lodges, namely: Ayr, Dundee, Dunfermline, Edinburgh, Glasgow and Stirling.

William Schaw and his associate Alexander Dickson further decided that the art of memory should be a necessary qualification for membership of masonic lodges.

The reason for this qualification was to encourage mystical enlightenment and, most likely, the memorising of the Old Charges. The art of memory is also a requirement in the performance and delivery of modern masonic rituals.

The first recognised lodge in Scotland was Edinburgh, Kilwinning was the second and Stirling was third. There may be some confusion as to the oldest lodge for although the minutes of Kilwinning go back to 1642, it is recorded by Bernard Jones that the Edinburgh Lodge minutes go back to 1599.

It is interesting to note that Stirling was not listed as one of the nine founding members of Scotland's Grand Lodge even though there are references to it being active in 1599.

Stevenson records that the first Grand Master of Scotland, William St Clair, was a Catholic, had a mistress, and generally was not accepted by the majority. He eventually went to live in Ireland for the rest of his life.

However, his son and heir William, was appreciated by all. He was knighted in 1617, married the daughter of the Archbishop of Glasgow and became the Sheriff of the Shire of Edinburgh in 1622.

Sir Anthony Alexander, who succeeded Schaw as the Master of Works to the King, was succeeded by his brother Henry in 1637, much to the dislike of the St Clairs.

Sir William St Clair died in 1650, during the period of civil war between England and Scotland, however, the St Clair of Roslin maintained their position through their heirs and were obliged to receive the Masonic Word in 1697.

Stevenson further records that during the civil war, three senior artillery officers joined the Lodge of Edinburgh. This highlights the fact that William Schaw and his successors were not just Master of Works but also Master Gunners.

During the 25-year period between 1590 and 1615, there was a recognisable increase in the number of references to non-operative masonic lodges, namely: Dunfermline 1701, Hamilton, which became Hamilton Kilwinning 1701, Haughfoot 1702, and the Lodge of Dumfries in 1712.

Other lodges referred to in the 18th century were Canongate, Canongate Kilwinning, Kirkcudbright, Leith, Linlithgow and Scone. Towards the end of the century, there is evidence of many more lodges from extant minutes, namely: Aberdeen, Aitchison's Haven, Banff, Dumfries, Dunblane, Hamilton, Haughfoot, Inverness, Kelso and Kilmolymack; Aitchison's Haven and Haughfoot no longer exist.

Stevenson, therefore, contends that William Shaw was the founder of Freemasonry, but it can only relate to that form of Freemasonry included in his statutes. It is more than likely that earlier forms of Freemasonry were practised prior to the publication of those statutes, some of which may have influenced later versions.

The following Scottish Masonic lodges (pre–1710) are listed by dates of their earliest references:

1.	Aitchison's Haven –	9 January	1599
2.	Edinburgh –	31 July	1599
3.	St Andrews –	27 November	1599
4.	Kilwinning –	28 December	1599
5.	Stirling –	28 December	1599
6.	Haddington –		1599
7.	Dunfermline –		1600/1
8.	Glasgow –	31 December	1613
9.	Dundee –		1627/8
10.	Linlithgow –	2 March	1654
11.	Scone (Perth) –	24 December	1658
12.	Aberdeen –		1670
13.	Melrose –	28 December	1674
14.	Canongate Kilwinning –	20 December	1677
15.	Inverness –	27 December	1678
16.	Dumfries –	20 May	1687
17.	Canongate and Leith –	29 May	1688
18.	Kirkcudbright –		c. 1691
19.	Hamilton –	25 March	1695
20.	Dunblane –	April	1695
21.	Kelso –	2 June	1701
22.	Haughfoot –	22 December	1702
23.	Banff –		1703
24.	Kilmolymock (Elgin) –	27 December	1704
25.	Edinburgh Journeymen –		1707–12
26.	Hamilton Kilwinning –		1730
27.	Old Kilwinning St John, Inverness		1737
28.	Dunbar Castle –		1758
29.	Keith, No 56, Peterhead –		1789

Earliest Masonic Lodges in England

1.	Warrington	1646
2.	Chester	1673
3.	York No. 4	1693
4.	Alnwick, Northumberland	1779

Harry Carr in his work 'Early Masonic Catechisms' gives a slightly different list:

Lodge of Edinburgh	1598
Lodge of Aitchison's Haven	1598
Lodge of Aberdeen	1670
Trinity College, Dublin	1724

In the above book, Harry Carr states, *Gentlemen Masons in Scotland were received into lodges of operative masons with the same ceremonies as working masons. Gentlemen masons in England were originally received into lodges of accepted masons with similar ceremonies as those that prevailed in lodges of operative masons in Scotland.*

In the case of occasional or semi-permanent lodges of accepted masons, which have been traced to the 17th or early 18th century London, Warrington, Chester, York and Scarborough, there is evidence to suggest that a version of the MS Constitutions played a part in the ceremonies of admission.

It is understood that all pre–1710 Scottish lodges were initially operative as they were closely tied to the trade of stonemasons. However, with the evolving change to speculative Freemasonry, many distinguished gentlemen became members of the fraternity in the 1730s, including Bro Frederick, His Royal Highness the Prince of Wales, Son of George II and Father of George III.

Michael Baigent & Richard Leigh in their book 'The Temple and the Lodge' explain that when *the Grand Lodge was created in 1717, (initially known as the Premier Grand Lodge of Freemasonry) it was created in large part as a Whig or Hanoverian attempt to break what had hitherto been a virtual Jacobite monopoly. The date chosen was 24th June, St John's Day, the day formerly held sacred by the (Knights) Templars.*

The 24 June is also midsummer's day when the sun rises in the northeast thus illuminating the northeast corner of a building, which is symbolically where the first or foundation stone is laid in accordance with masonic ritual.

In order to regularise Freemasonry, the four London lodges agreed to amalgamate to found a Grand Lodge in 1717. By doing so this enabled them to break the overpowering Jacobite influence.

The attraction of a Grand Lodge drew more lodges into the fold and by 1723, the number had risen to 52, many having pre-dated the founding. The Grand Lodge of England first met in the London tavern named the 'Goose and Gridiron' in St Paul's Churchyard.

Grand Lodge now governed the three Craft degrees in Freemasonry and any practice of the higher degrees, which originated in Jacobite Freemasonry, were put on the back burner until after the Jacobite Rebellion in 1745. This is the rebellion that culminated in the Jacobites being defeated at the Battle of Culloden.

In 1723 James Anderson produced his non-political 'Constitutions', which became the Bible of English Freemasonry. The Rev. James Anderson was born and grew up in Aberdeen and was ordained into the Church of Scotland in 1707 before moving to London where he remained for the rest of his life.

The preamble to the Constitutions was written by John Desaguliers, who had political connections to the inner circle of the Grand Lodge and subsequently had a significant influence on the direction of Freemasonry.

Baigent & Leigh continue, *The constitutions made Grand Lodge respectable and an unimpugnable social and cultural adjunct of the Hanoverian regime that was to extend, eventually, up to the throne. In England, the Grand Lodge established something approaching a monopoly; and its political orthodoxy was subsequently never seriously in doubt.*

In the years following John Theophilus Desaguliers' visit in 1721, lodges in Scotland assumed a speculative complexion; in some of them the bare ceremony was replaced during the following two decades by the fuller and more dramatic ceremonies borrowed from the south, and within 15 years, by 1736, Scotland had founded its own Grand Lodge much on the English pattern.

Kenneth O'Morgan records in his 'Oxford Illustrated History of Britain' that by the early 1730s Horace Walpole was faced with a dangerous alliance of rivals at court. When Walpole attempted to extend the excise system, which was financially sound, but detested by many, it gave the opposition the opportunity they had been waiting for.

Walpole, realising the danger, withdrew the scheme in 1733 and saved his administration for the time being. In the general election of 1734, he suffered a widespread reaction to his policies, severely reducing his majority in the Commons.

Walpole was finally brought down in 1739, following an aggressive stance favoured by the Tories towards the Spanish empire that had the support of Frederick, the Prince of Wales, Son of George II.

The alliance of alienated Tories, discontented Whigs, hostile businessmen and the heir to the throne created a dangerous situation, which forced Walpole into a war, of which he was not in favour.

This was the War of the Austrian Succession 1740–1748, which wrought Britain not just against Spain, but against a powerful Bourbon coalition.

King George II, who had given his support to Walpole, made it his primary concern to protect his electorate but this was not conducive to his domestic interests and the need to invest in an army to fight in Germany and the Netherlands proved to be unpopular.

Thus, bringing Walpole's prediction that warfare would mean a struggle for English succession on English soil and so it proved.

The full extent of the danger to the Hanoverian dynasty was brought to a head by the Jacobite invasion of 1745. The English army had been neglected and was no longer a force to be reckoned with.

However, the alarm and panic raised by this invasion encouraged the English to rally to the crisis and defeat the invading Jacobite army at Culloden, much to the relief of the government. O'Morgan records that the crisis of 1745, provided a useful corrective to the complacency of the Whig system.

Eight years after the Battle of Culloden, the aftermath was still being felt, for in 1753, there is a record of a Jacobite rebel being publicly hanged in London.

The Young Pretender, Charles Edward Stuart, the grandson of James II of England/James VII of Scotland, who had laid claim to the throne, led the Jacobites but, after he was defeated at Culloden, he fled to France to remain in exile for the rest of his life and the Jacobite threat was finally extinguished.

This subsequently allowed political stability to return. The conventional accounts of the immense economic growth and change, born out of the Industrial Revolution, locate its birth firmly in the mid–18th century and coincided with the death throes of Jacobitism.

William Pitt the Elder is best known as the wartime political leader of Britain in the Seven Year's War (1756–1763), especially for his single-minded devotion to victory over France, a victory which ultimately solidified Britain's dominance over world affairs.

The Seven Year War was a global conflict involving Europe, the Americas, West Africa, India and the Philippines.

Pitt is also known for his popular appeal, his opposition to corruption in government, his support for the advocacy of British greatness, expansionism and colonialism, and his antagonism towards Britain's chief enemies and rivals for colonial power, Spain and France.

It is argued that his statesmanship was based on a clear, consistent, and distinct appreciation of the value of the empire. He died in 1779 before his son took on the mantle.

William Hague in his biography of 'William Pitt the Younger' commented:

The Jacobite attempts to restore the Stuarts to the throne in place of the Hanoverians, in both 1715 and 1745–46, had been assisted by Catholic powers, specifically France and Spain. To the great majority of people in England, it was therefore unthinkable to allow Catholics to hold office.

Far beyond the church and parliament, Catholicism meant to most people treachery, invasion, bloodshed and persecution. Any acceptance that Catholics could have the rights and privileges of other Englishmen was therefore pandering to foreigners, in particular the French, thus returning to Jacobite sympathies and destroying a fundamental attribute of Englishness.

The fear of the Jacobites had kept the suspect Tories out of office for a generation, and the Whigs, who prided themselves on the 1688 Settlement, were permanently in power from 1714 to the 1760s.

The conquest of Quebec changed such thinking for it brought vast numbers of Catholics of French descent into the British Empire and the objection to Roman Catholicism began to be relaxed.

English Freemasonry by the 1730s, had become strongly associated with the social and cultural establishments under the direction of the Grand Lodge influencing great reformers in both England and other countries around the world, particularly France and America.

This was further elaborated by Baigent & Leigh when they recorded:

Grand Lodge suffused the whole of English society and inculcated its values into the very fabric of English thought. Insisting on a universal brotherhood, which transcended national frontiers. Freemasonry was to exert a profound influence on the great reformers of the 18th century, namely: David Hume in England, Voltaire, Diderot, Montesquieu and Rousseau in France and on their disciples in what was to become the United States.

During the 18th century, England's class system became more flexible and more embracing than anywhere else in Europe.

This was reflected in the ethos of Grand Lodge, where antisemitism was discredited with many Jews becoming freemasons and taking an active part in public life. By the freeing up of prejudice, the middle classes successfully expanded their commercial and industrial businesses to the financial benefit of the government.

These changes also led to the creation of welfare programmes including the charitable provision for widows and orphans. It is also thought that Freemasonry, together with the medieval guilds, were the forerunner of the trade unions.

During this period, pro-Jacobite lodges in England were driven underground, although some persisted, particularly in the north-east around Newcastle and at the Radclyffe family estates at Derwentwater, for there was little latitude for expansion or development in the prevailing climate.

Likewise, in Scotland where much evidence pertaining to Freemasonry between 1689 and 1745 was lost, deliberately or otherwise, due to the failure of the rebellion. The situation in Ireland was quite different.

The early history of the Grand Lodge of Ireland is thin. Their first Grand Master was the Duke of Montague, who in 1721, had presided over the Grand Lodge of England. Montague was the godson of George I and staunchly pro-Hanoverian. Baigent and Leigh record that between 1725 and 1731, there is a total lacuna in its history.

Later, commentators concluded it must have been hopelessly split between Hanoverian supporters and Jacobites. Consequently, the Irish Grand Lodge became and remained a repository for aspects of Freemasonry, which the Grand Lodge of England repudiated or disowned.

It was to this form of Freemasonry that the numerous British regiments, passing through Ireland or stationed there in garrison, were exposed. Most of the regimental field lodges were initially warranted by the Irish Grand Lodge, as they were not at this time accepted by the English constitution.

This later changed, but it was many more years before they were accepted, which had serious implications for the ritual adopted around the world.

The presence of regimental field lodges at this early stage reflects the importance of Freemasonry to the military that remains to this day. Although most of the early field lodges were subsequently erased, the regiments replaced them with permanent lodges.

Baigent & Leigh continue, *Freemasonry seems to have come to France with the contingents of the defeated Jacobite army between 1688 and 1691. According to one 18th century account, the first lodge in France dates from 25 March 1688, and was established by an infantry regiment, the Royal Irish, which had been formed by Charles II in 1661.*

But if Freemasonry first came to France in 1688, some 35 years were to elapse before the first authoritatively documented native French lodge was established. This was formed in 1725 or 1726. Its primary founder was Charles Radclyffe, Earl of Derwentwater, whose elder brother, James, had been executed for his part in the 1715 rebellion.

However, Dr Ric Berman records in his recent article, published in *Freemasonry Today*, entitled '*Consequences of the 1723 Constitutions part 2*: France', that two masonic lodges were established in Paris in 1726.

These were followed by many others throughout the country namely in, Valenciennes, Lyons, Rouen, le Havre, Pau, Nantes, Caen, Bordeaux, Aubigny, Avignon, Montpelier, Marseilles and Bayonne. It should be noted that the first golf club in France was established at Pau; could there be a connection?

It has been established that by 1729 Freemasonry in France was growing apace and through Charles Radclyffe became linked to the Jacobite system of Freemasonry. This led in 1773 to the foundation of the Grand Orient, which eventually became the most important Freemasonic body in France.

The situation of Freemasonry in France became the focus of two major speeches given by a Scotsman, Andrew Michael Ramsay, on the occasion of Radclyffe assuming the role of the Grand Master of French Freemasonry.

The first of these speeches, which was to become one of the major landmarks in Freemasonic history, became known as 'Ramsay's Oration'.

In his speech, Ramsay declared, *"The world is nothing but a huge republic of which every nation is a family and every individual a child."*

This statement was influential to later political thinkers in Europe and the American colonies.

Following the second oration made on 1 August 1737, Freemasonry was declared to be innocent of 'indecency', but potentially dangerous *by virtue of the indifference of the order towards religions.*

On 2 August, Freemasonry became forbidden in France, and their grand secretary was arrested. Following police raids, many documents and membership lists were confiscated but not before Cardinal Fleury became aware of the extraordinary number of high-ranking nobles and churchmen who were listed as freemasons.

This action caused Rome to be alarmed, encouraging Fleury to apply pressure on his administrators to take action against those engaged in Freemasonry. In 1738, Pope Clement XII issued a Papal Bull, *in eminenti apostulatus specula*, forbidding Catholics to become freemasons under the threat of excommunication.

Two years later, this was extended to being punishable by death. The result of this dramatic action was to topple the Jacobites from their position of supremacy in France, thus affecting the evolution of its doctrine. This resulted in the Grand Orient emerging as the Premier Grand Lodge of France.

Likewise in England, the influence of religion and politics was excluded from Freemasonry, which now realigned itself with the virtues of moderation, tolerance and flexibility, finding no conflict with the Anglican church. Indeed, many of its clergy were freemasons.

However, in Europe, which was mainly Catholic, Freemasonry gave birth to a repository for revolutionary sentiment and activity.

It is quite clear that during the 18th century, Freemasonry became well established in England, Ireland and Scotland and, through colonial settlers and the militia, it began to take root in Europe and on the continent of America.

Subsequently, our modern educational institutions, trade associations and professional bodies began to adopt the core traditions of Freemasonry, which pervade to this day.

Chapter Three
Early Golf Clubs and Societies

Many historians of Freemasonry have made no secret of their belief that there was a strong connection between the idea of the first Grand Lodge in 1717 and the ethos of a club.

In the late 17th and early 18th centuries, masonic gatherings could certainly be described as convivial affairs. G W Speth, a founding member of the *Quatuor Coronati*, believed that the lodges of accepted masons included some mystic ceremony, but apart from that they were convivial societies.

Lodges met in taverns, these being the customary meeting places of the day, thus, in the taverns, coffee and chocolate houses, the ethos of a club was born.

This is further elaborated on by David Stevenson in his 'Origins of Freemasonry' where he records that in 1688 the Royal Company of Archers are referred (to) in Kilwinning as the social occupation in which a number of masons were involved.

The Company of Archers most likely offered an alternative means for socialising and dining. This implies the early formation of an exclusive club and is one of the earliest indications of the military being involved.

Earliest Golf Sites and Golfers

The earliest references to golf prior to the 16th century were to its being banned or condemned in favour of archery practise. The ban was lifted in 1502. Thereafter, golf was played throughout Scotland from 1502. At that time, there were only two sites in England and these were at Greenwich and Richmond.

The earliest golf sites are:

1502 Perth	The Royal Golfer
1503 Falkland Palace	The Courtier Golfer
1505 Stirling Castle	The Royal Golfer
1527 Carnoustie	The Links Golfer
1562 Montrose	The Schoolboy Golfer
1574 St Andrews	The Student Golfer
1606 Richmond	
1608 Greenwich Park	The Prince Golfer
1617 Fraserburgh	The Miscreant Golfer
1617 Dunbar	More Miscreant Golfers
1619 Dornoch	The Young Earl Golfer
1619 Leith Links	The Bishop Golfer
1625 Aberdeen	The Schoolmaster Golfer
1650 Gullane	The Weaver Golfers
1672 Musselburgh & Seton House	The Lawyer Golfer
1672 North Berwick	The Law Lord Golfer
1672 Elgin & Burghead	The MP Golfer
1702 Fortrose	The Farmer Golfer
1711 Bruntsfield Links	The Poet Golfer
1721 Glasgow Green	The Non-Playing Partner

All of the above relate to the links form of golf and not the churchyard version. Early golf in Scotland had two distinct versions. One was a target game in the countryside, around churchyards and village greens, hitting balls at targets such as stakes or trees. The other version was played on the links and is the forerunner of today's game.

In considering the oldest golf courses as opposed to golf clubs, the 19 oldest golf courses in the British Isles are:

1754 St Andrews Old Course (1552)
1787 Elie and Earlsferry (1589)
1817 Scotscraig
1818 Montrose North Links
1823 Kingsbarns
1830 Musselburgh Old Course (1672)
1832 North Berwick West Links
1835 Carnoustie
1840 Gullane Links (1 & 2)
1845 Monifieth Links
1846 Leven Links
1851 Prestwick
1851 Lanark
1856 Dunbar Links
1857 The Curragh, Ireland
1860 Perth North Inch
1864 Westward Ho!
1868 Leven and Lundin Links

This list differs quite widely from that of the oldest golf societies because all courses except St Andrews and Earlsferry had to relocate late in the 19th century to create an 18-hole course.

The right to play golf on the links is enshrined in the 16th century Burgh records of St Andrews (1552) and Elie (1589). At Musselburgh, the play was first recorded in 1672. The first mention of links golf being played is on Barry Links, Carnoustie. Whereas the first mention of a golf hole is at Aberdeen in 1625 on the Old Aberdeen Links.

Some of the above-listed golf courses do not reflect local interest in the game, i.e. Pau and Westward Ho! The game here was developed with the support of prominent London golfers; likewise, at Wimbledon Common, which was founded in 1865, and at Haddington and Brook Common.

Whilst it is recognised that golf was first recorded in England at Blackheath (Greenwich), there are other early sightings as explained by Neil S Miller in his article 'Early Golf in England (1606–1659)'.

In this, he states, *Reliable evidence exists to indicate that during the first half of the 17th century golf was being played at several identifiable locations in England, the earliest of which appears to be Richmond in Surrey.*

The available evidence supports the conclusion that the game of golf was exported from Scotland to England around the time that James VI of Scotland acceded to the throne of England in 1603 (where he became James I of England).

Where the identity of the golfers can be established, a pattern emerges of early golf in England being a game that was played initially by royalty at Richmond in 1606, (Greenwich 1608,) and nobility at Royston in 1624, and subsequently by the gentry at Westminster in 1659.

Vis:	1606	Richmond, Surrey	Prince Henry Stuart
	1608	Greenwich	King James I of England
	1624	Royston, Hertfordshire	Duke of Buckingham and Sir Robert Deal
	1646	Newcastle, Northumberl'd	King Charles I
	1655	London	Lord Strathnavar
	1659	Tothill Fields, Westminster	'The Gentry'

There is a long and established tradition that golf was played in the vicinity of Greenwich and Blackheath shortly after the arrival in London of James I's court in 1603.

Indeed, given the number of Scots that came south with James I, it could be seen as inevitable that golf would have been played at numerous different locations, e.g. in the history of the London Scottish Golf Club it has been argued that there is no reason to suppose that golf was not played in an informal game by individuals on Wimbledon Common from the time the game was brought south by James VI (I).

In the same way, it is certainly possible that Greenwich or Blackheath was one of the locations at which the earliest golf in England was played but locating documentary evidence has proved to be difficult.

The initial object of this research was to examine what influence Freemasonry had on the formation of golf clubs and subsequently, the role that the militia played during this formative period.

In the 17th century, there was no formal army in the British Isles other than private armies in the pay of the aristocracy, many of whom were members of the early golf clubs and the masonic fraternity. It is, therefore, necessary to examine and understand the history of the 17 oldest golf clubs and or societies; these are described as follows:

1608 Royal Blackheath GC, London.

Founded by James VI (I), who learnt the game of golf in Scotland. 1608 has always been recognised as the foundation of the Royal Blackheath Golf Club due to this being the earliest record of golf being played in England, but according to Neil S. Miller, *see above*, there is recent evidence of golf being played over the common at Richmond in 1606.

These dates relate to the migration of the Scottish King James VI who became King James I of England when he moved south with his entourage to Greenwich Palace. It was his entourage who were keen golfers and used the heath at Greenwich to continue their sport.

The first evidence of formalised golf is recorded as 1745, but the club was not established until 1766. It moved to its current location at Eltham, London, in 1923.

Although the date of 1608 is generally accepted, there has been no documentary evidence to support it. It was not until 1766, when Mr Henry Lamb donated a silver club to be played for as a trophy, that there was any evidence of a golf club being in existence. The precedence for such a trophy being gifted is recorded at Leith in 1744.

The first winner of the silver club at Blackheath was Alexander Duncan in 1766. Duncan hailed from Edinburgh and he had been Captain of the St Andrews Society in 1756 and 1761. He was also an active member of 'The Gentlemen Golfers' at Leith and a prominent Scottish freemason.

Ian Henderson & David Stirk in their history of 'Royal Blackheath' expand further on the role of freemasons in golf societies by stating:

They (Societies) had club uniforms, ceremonies, fines in the form of drinks for absence or other offences; toasts, including the Masonic three times three. When necessary new membership was controlled with the use of the black ball.

Attendance at dinners and guests were recorded, as were often details of the meals. There was never a great deal in those days to mention about golf, except the bets on matches, which were usually entered in a separate book and were by no means all related to golf.

1735 the Royal Burgess Club, Musselburgh Links; known as the Royal Burgess Golfing Society of Edinburgh.

There is no documentary evidence of the Edinburgh Golfing Society being formed in 1735. Initially, they played at Bruntsfield Links, Edinburgh and met in Maggie Johnstone's tavern and later at 'The Golfhall'.

In 1773, 16 new members were admitted of which a few of them were Burgesses. The leader of this group was Orlando Hart, who was elected the society's first captain. During the early period, they met in various hostelries but from 1813 they settled upon *The Golf House* tavern, formerly *The Golfhall* which was owned by club-maker Thomas Comb.

It was also known amongst the society as a *society hall*.

'The minute' written in 1735 by three members of the Society, namely Daniel Kerr, Alexander Milne and Charles

Rhind, suggests that they were endeavouring to keep the old society alive by amending the rules to permit a wider form of entry, most probably those who were not freemasons.

However, it should be noted that at the time Daniel Kerr, the Secretary, and Charles Rhind, the Treasurer, were both Freemasons.

It is interesting to note that the Burgess Club was founded in 1735, one year before the foundation of the Grand Lodge of Scotland, which may explain why, if it was an official lodge, they were not recognised or included in the Register of the Grand Lodge of Scotland.

There is little doubt of the masonic origins of the club. Their name and present-day tradition of *shaking in* new members, whereby the Captain of the Burgess can admit anyone on the shake of his hand, admits of little other interpretation.

In the early days, the Captain was allowed to admit three (masonic) members on the shake of a hand whilst others referred to a masonic initiation that new members went through before being allowed to join. It is believed that the Jacobite members of Royal Burgess were supporters of the claim of Bonnie Prince Charlie.

In 1873, the Society amalgamated with Musselburgh New Golf Club and made its home at Musselburgh Links under the leadership of their Captain, James Moore SSC. However, in 1894 the Burgess Society moved to Barnton Park where Robert Clark, an Edinburgh publishing magnate, golf author and R&A gold medallist, had developed a 9-hole course on land owned by the Maitland family.

The Society became the Royal Burgess in 1929 before King George V ordered it to be changed to the Royal Burgess

Golfing Society of Edinburgh. They have remained at Barnton since 1895.

The members of the Society wore a uniform of scarlet jackets with black collars, similar to Royal Blackheath, and had social dinners after playing golf, but these gradually died out. It is further recorded that as late as 1838 the masonic *three times three* toast was still being drunk.

David Stirk adds from his 'Golf—the History of an Obsession' that the *masonic connection is clear from the records of the society, whose captain was allowed to elect three new members a year* on the shake of the hand *and those members agreed to purchase three-dozen masonic aprons. The records also refer to members going through the ordeal bravely and giving all the right answers.*

Once the membership started to grow, many of the new members were enthusiastic golfers but not freemasons and this made it difficult for a club (society) to continue as a masonic lodge. By then the freemasons, by their strong discipline, had already set up properly organised golf clubs, keen and fair competitions, and formal rules of play.

1744 The Honourable Company of Edinburgh Golfers, Musselburgh.

The Gentlemen Golfers of Leith, now the HCEG, started playing at Leith Links in 1744. The foundation date for this club relates to a committee meeting held in 1744, comprised of Gentlemen Golfers of Edinburgh who drafted the first 13 rules of golf to enable them to compete for a silver club, presented to them by the City of Edinburgh.

John Rattray was one of those who helped draw up the first rules of golf, which were adopted by the Society of St Andrews Golfers a year later, and form the basis of the rules of golf today. The new legislation also introduced the ballot box and the *black ball*.

The competition for the silver club was to be played over the Leith Links, a course of 5-holes. The first winner was John Rattray, a physician and champion archer who, as the winner, was declared Captain of golf for the ensuing year.

Consequently, members of the Society had to be carefully vetted and approved before they were admitted. This was the first known organised golf competition.

The City of Edinburgh had previously gifted a Silver Arrow to the Royal Company of Archers and felt inspired to do the same for the Gentlemen Golfers. The golfers competing for the first silver club were:

John Rattray	Hew Dalrymple
Robert Biggar	James Gordon
James Carmichael	Hon. James Leslie
Richard Cockburn	George Suttie
William Crosse	James Veith
David Dalrymple	

Duncan Forbes was also due to play but did not compete. The book containing the entries was kept at 'Luckie Clephanes'. All were important and well-known people in Edinburgh and nearly all were freemasons. Robert Biggar was the publican at Golfhall, the world's, first clubhouse at Bruntsfield, 20 years earlier.

The competition was to be played annually and was open to all golfers but by 1764, it became limited to the members of the Leith Club.

Duncan Forbes who was the President of the Honourable Company of Edinburgh Golfers signed the first regular minutes of the Company.

Their golf was played by all classes on common land owned by Edinburgh Council but after their game, the Gentlemen Golfers retired to Luckie Clephane's where they dined and wined in great conviviality with speechmaking and songs being a significant part of the evening.

The wearing of uniforms was obligatory and fines were imposed for failure to comply and for other breaches of discipline. Their extensive and detailed wager book was kept at Luckie Clephane's.

The suitability of their club premises was challenged by the members and Alastair J Johnston and James F Johnston in the chapter on 'Golf and the Freemasons 1766–1775', from 'The Chronicles of Golf 1457–1857', state that, *In 1767, the Gentlemen Golfer at Leith considered the premises they frequented had become inappropriate for social gatherings of the Society as well as the storage of golf equipment and new premises were sought.*

A petition was presented to Edinburgh town council, by William St Clair of Roslyn, for a new purpose-built clubhouse and the Leith Society granted a feu to construct the world's first custom-built golf clubhouse.

22 of the Gentlemen Golfers contributed £25 each to provide the funding and the foundation stone was laid in 1768 in the SE corner by three strokes with the mallet *in the presence of the Captain of the Society, Alexander Keith.*

All of the 22 were (free)masons and William St Clair was the (hereditary) Grand Master Mason of Scotland at that time; Alexander Duncan numbered in the 22. It is also recorded in an article by Bobby Burt, that they were all dressed in masonic uniforms.

It is probable that it was the intention of the parties concerned to construct, not only an amenity to service the members of the golfing society but also to provide a facility to host the activities of the local masonic lodge. On occasions, the rituals of both entities would be indistinguishable because of the coincidence of membership in the two organisations.

The Gentlemen Golfers built the clubhouse in 1768, having previously met in Luckie Clephane's tavern on Kirkgate; sadly, it is now demolished.

The Honourable Company had a strong masonic influence in the early years and the foundation stone of the clubhouse was laid with masonic tradition, however, it is postured that the laying of the foundation stone in this manner does not indicate the heavy hand of Freemasonry beyond the fact that it dates from a time when Freemasonry was strong and highly regarded.

It merely indicates that many important people who were involved with golf were freemasons and acknowledged as such. A notice describing the occasion is set out below:

This day William St Clair of Roslin Esq., the undoubted representative of the Honourable and Heritable GMM (Grand Master Mason) of Scotland, in the presence of Alexander Keith Esq., Captain of the Honourable Company of Golfers, and other worthy members of the golfing company, all Masons, the GM now in his Grand Climax of Golfing, laid the foundation of the golfing house in the SE corner thereof, by three strokes with the mallet.
Alexr Keith C
Wm St Clair GMM

It was recorded by Alastair and James Johnston in their chapter on 'Golf and the Freemasons 1766–1775', from the 'Chronicles of Golf 1457–1857' that, *William St Clair, when he was Captain of the Gentlemen Golfers in 1771, the Society had his portrait painted in full length and in his golfing attire by Sir George Chambers at the expense of the Society.*

The painting now hangs in the Hall of the Royal Company of Archers, and a replica, painted by J A Ford, hangs in the Muirfield clubhouse.

They continue that, *William St Clair first competed for the silver club at Leith in 1751 and consequent to his subsequent victories in that competition, he was Captain of the Society in 1761, 1766, 1770 and 1771. In addition, he earned the Captaincy of the St Andrews Society in 1764, 1766 and 1768, the same year as he was declared the Grand Master Mason of Scotland.*

Their masonic connection continues for Alexander McDougall, who was elected Secretary of the Gentlemen

Golfers at Leith and was also the Grand Secretary of the Grand Lodge of Scotland.

In an article by Bobby Burt, concerning the clubhouses of the Honourable Company of Edinburgh Golfers (HCEG) entitled *'Leith to Muirfield via Musselburgh'*, Bobby Burt states that, *There was one formally established group, the Royal Company of Archers, comprised of Scottish noblemen and formed in 1676, who, intent on preserving their archery skills, practised on the Links of Leith. But it was not until the 18th century 'Period of Enlightenment' in Edinburgh that men of like-minded intellect, social status, standing, and interests formed clubs and societies, many with arcane rules and shibboleths. It was this group of well-to-do Edinburgh archery and golf addicts, known by a variety of informal names involving random juxtaposition of the words Edinburgh, Leith, Gentlemen, Golfers, who formed a club and played over the links.*

In Edinburgh, inns and taverns were established under the reign of King James I and archers and golfers would eat and drink at these inns when they practised or played. In Leith, the street known as Kirkgate boasted many inns and taverns close to the links. Kinnaird's was still extant in 1932 but the Red Lyon, in the middle of Kirkgate, burned down. However, in 1734, archery was banned from practising at Leith and they moved back to Edinburgh where they conducted their practise sessions, first on Bruntsfield Links and then on East Meadows. (This is) where they patronised Mrs Balfour's tavern at Louriston Yeards.

The first two homes were Luckie Clephane's and Straiton's and it is well documented that the archers and golfers patronised these two taverns. Straiton's was the preferred house prior to the building of a golf house and it is noted that William St Clair of Roslyn was frequently seen there. Luckie Clephane's tavern was located at the bottom of Easter Road. Straiton's was a tavern at the head of the Kirkgate, on the west side facing Laurie Street leading to the Links.

In 1831, the Honourable Company fell into financial difficulties and an administrator was appointed. This resulted in their early treasures being sold off to clear the debts, but this was not enough, so the Leith clubhouse was sold.

There were no competitions held during this troubled four-year period but after their finances had been settled, in 1836 the Honourable Company moved to Musselburgh. They continued to play on the Musselburgh Links and played also on the West Links at North Berwick.

They used Mrs McKendrick's Inn as a temporary clubhouse, which later became the Musselburgh Arms Hotel.

They built a new clubhouse in 1865 in Links Place, Musselburgh, which has its current address as 8 Balcarres Road.

Burt continues, that it was *built of grey stone, and all four buildings remain today, although No. 8 is now shared by an infant's nursery and a masonic lodge, the presence of the latter confirming that, as at Leith, the foundation cornerstone was laid in masonic tradition.*

They later moved again, due to overcrowding, to the site of the East Lothian racecourse where Old Tom Morris designed their new course, Muirfield, which opened in 1891 and is still in use today. It is regularly used as one of The Open venues.

1754 The Royal & Ancient Golf Club of St Andrews.

The location of the old course at St Andrews has not changed throughout its history. In the Middle Ages, golf became a popular sport, and it has been played over the links of St Andrews for the last 600 years.

King James II of Scotland, banned it from the links in 1457, as it was thought to be distracting to the practise of archery, but in 1502 when James IV became a golfer the ban was lifted.

The course on which they played in 1754 consisted of 11 holes out and 11 holes in with the same hole being used in both directions!

However, it was decided that the first and last four holes were too short and that these should be changed to two holes instead of four, with the remaining 16 holes being played to double greens. Hence, the standard 18-hole course was established for all time.

The links that were in the ownership of St Andrews town council were sold in 1797 to raise money in support of a failing council and it was purchased by local merchants who converted it to a rabbit farm. This led to open warfare between the farmers and the golfers.

Ultimately, in 1821 James Cheape of Strathyrum, a local landowner and keen golfer, bought the links and restored their use to the playing of golf.

The Royal & Ancient Golf Club was founded in 1754 as the Society of St Andrews Golfers. The first use of the term society of golfers occurs in the minutes of 1770.

The initial membership comprised 22 noblemen, professors and landowners who contributed to a silver club that had the St Andrews cross on its head, which was to be played for annually over the links.

The regulations and conditions of entry were almost identical to those that were laid down by the Honourable Company of Edinburgh Golfers (HCEG) 10 years earlier. The first winner was Baillie William Lansdale, who by winning became their Captain for the year. The initial 22 members were:

> The Rt. Hon. Charles 5th Earl of Elgin and 9th Earl of Kincardine, Grand Master Mason of Scotland 1761–1763
> The Rt. Hon. James 5th Earl of Wemyss, Grand Master Mason of Scotland 1743–1744
> The Hon. Thomas Leslie, son of 9th Earl of Rothes
> The Hon. James Leslie, son of 9th Earl of Rothes
> The Hon. Francis Charteris, son of 7th Earl of Wemyss, Grand Master Mason of Scotland 1747–1748
> Sir James Wymess, Baronet MP
> Sir Robert Henderson, Baronet
> Lieutenant-General James St Clair MP
> David Scot of Scotstarvet MP
> James Oswald of Dunnikier
> David Young, Professor of Philosophy
> James Lumsdain Esq. Provost of St Andrews
> James Wemyss of Weemyss Hall
> Walter Wemyss of Lathockar
> John Bethune of Blebo
> Henry Bethune of Clato
> Thomas Spens the Younger of Lathallan

James Cheape of Sauchie
Arthur Martin of Milntoun, a Fifeshire 6aird
Maurice Trent of Pitcullo, son of Leith merchants
Robert Douglas Esq. Solicitor of Edinburgh
John Young, Professor of Philosophy

According to David Stirk in his 'Golf—History and Tradition':

The Hon. Francis Charteris of Amisfield was elected to the Royal Company of Archers in 1747 and Captain of the R&A in 1765.

James Leslie won the Silver Arrow at the University of St Andrews in 1720.

Lieutenant-General James St Clair was the nephew of William St Clair of Roslyn and succeeded to the family estate when William died but not the hereditary title of Grand Master Mason.

Thomas Spens was a very senior member of the Royal Company of Archers.

The Right Hon. Charles 9th Earl of Kincardine was a member of the Bruce family who were members of the Royal Company of Archers and Freemasons, one of their (family) members becoming the Grand Master Mason of Scotland in 1961–1965.

John Rattray, (who is not listed as one of the 22 initial members,) was a surgeon in Edinburgh, a freemason and was elected to the Royal Company of Archers. He won the Silver Arrow of that company in 1735 and 1744.

He was also a Jacobite and nearly lost his life after the Battle of Culloden but was saved by an anti-Jacobite friend, who was also a masonic brother, Duncan Forbes.

William St Clair of Roslyn had a great influence on both the Royal Company of Archers and the HCEG and laid the foundation stone of the clubhouse at Leith for the HCEG and the foundation stone for Archers Hall in Edinburgh.

Duncan Forbes was a member of the Royal Company of Archers in 1710 when he was an advocate. He later became the Lord President of the Court of Session with the title Lord Forbes of Culloden. He was an anti-Jacobite and played a big but discreet part in saving his fellow masons after the Battle of Culloden.

In the chapter on '*Golf and the Freemasons 1766–1775*' from *'The Chronicles of Golf 1457–1857'* by Alastair J Johnston and James F Johnston it is stated that*:*

For the golfers of Leith and Bruntsfield, the attendant attractions of drinking and dining together after play had been a tradition that had been enjoyed at the hostelries of James Brownhill, Luckie Clephane and others since early in the 18th century.

Since its inception in 1754, however, the focus of the St Andrews Society seems to have been the advancement of the game itself. But, in 1766, a new emphasis on the social aspects of the club was recorded in the club minutes; a golf house at St Andrews, namely the tavern of Baillie Glass

On 4 May 1766, the Society agreed to meet fortnightly and to dine thereafter at Baillie Glass Inn. The annual competition for the silver club was initially open to all golfers but by 1773 it became limited to members only.

Baillie Glass Inn was later renamed the *Black Bull* Inn and, until the club had built their own clubhouse. The St Andrews golfers also used the *Cross Keys* hotel as an alternative for their dinners and the *Union Club* that overlooked the course. The current Royal & Ancient clubhouse was completed in 1854.

Angela Howe, the R&A's Director of Museum & Heritage added, "In some early golfing societies the masonic influence was strong (e.g. Gentlemen Golfers of Edinburgh and Blackheath) but this should not be overstated. Some of the customs were shared such as dining and drinking.

"However, when the foundation stone of the R&A's clubhouse was laid on 13 July 1853, by John Whyte Melville, who was a senior freemason, it was done with full masonic honours, starting with a procession from Madras College, accompanied by a band.

"The stone was hit with a mallet (three times) and Whyte Melville called upon the Great Architect of the Universe to shower down his blessing upon the work—"

It should be noted that John Whyte Melville became the Grand Master Mason of Scotland, 1864–1867.

It was not until King William IV agreed to be a patron of the Club in 1834, that the Society of St Andrews Golfers was renamed the Royal & Ancient Golf Club of St Andrews. The old course remained the only course in play until 1895 when the R&A built the new course. The Club maintained both courses until the early 1950s when they handed over the responsibility to The St Andrews Links Trust.

1761 Bruntsfield Golf Club, Musselburgh Links now the Bruntsfield Golfing Society.

The formation of the Bruntsfield Golfing Society dates from 1761. The Society played their golf over 5-holes at Bruntsfield Links, which lie in the shadow of Edinburgh Castle, although it is believed that golf had been played over these links since the 15th century.

The Links were open to all members of the public and became very congested, so much so that they began to play more of their golf over the Musselburgh Links. Their Autumn Meeting being held there since 1839.

The Society eventually moved to Musselburgh in 1876 where they built their own clubhouse in Golf Place, adjacent to the clubhouses of the Hon. Co. of Edinburgh Golfers, Edinburgh Burgess and Royal Musselburgh. Thus, with four established Clubs playing over the same ground, it again became very crowded.

In 1898, the Society sought a new venue at Davidsons' Mains on the Cramond Regis estate near Barnton. Willie Park Jnr laid out the new course. Dr Alister Mackenzie reconstructed it in 1922, James Braid in 1930 and Fred Hawtree in 1974.

They have been at Davidsons Mains, Edinburgh, since 1898; their new clubhouse being built in 1899, and is still in use today.

1774 Royal Musselburgh Golf Club, Musselburgh Links.

Royal Musselburgh is the only one of the oldest six Clubs for which no masonic link can be proved or inferred, although the oldest masonic lodge in the world, Aitchison's Haven, dating from 1599, met at locations very close to the Old Musselburgh course.

In 1774, the Silver Cup was won by Thomas MacMillan of Shorthope, who was most probably a founder member. Rev. Alexander Carlyle, who was also a founder member, won it in 1775.

The first minutes, which were recorded in Mrs Sherriff's Tavern in 1784, noted that:

Mr Gillies be elected as President

Mr Ramsay as Captain (most probably the 1784 Cup winner)

Mr Davidson as Secretary

Mr Brook as their officer (most probably a Steward or recorder of bets)

The Club met in various inns and taverns after matches for dinner in the afternoon or early evening where they arranged new matches and paid wagers due for those matches arranged at the previous dinner.

The results of all matches and bets were recorded and members who did not attend the dinners were fined.

Baillie, John Cochran, is recorded as keeper and surveyor of the Links in 1788. However, during the period 1797–1807, the Club was kept alive by Colonel Stewart acting as the custodian and Captain Sir John Hope, Bart, of Craighall, won the Silver Cup in 1807 and in 1812 it was won by Sir James G Baird, Bart.

Thereafter, between 1812 and 1827 Silver Cup was not competed. It was not until 1828, that Sir John Hope headed the revival of the Club and was again Captain that year; he subsequently became their President. The golf club moved to Prestonpans in 1922.

1777 Fraserburgh Golf Club (1891)

Founded in 1777, there is, however, documentary evidence of golf having been played at Fraserburgh in 1613. The Parish Kirk Session records refer to a young lad named John Gurnett who was chastised for *playing at the gouff* on a Sunday instead of going to church. He was ordered by the session to be sent to the *master's stool for correction*.

The most prominent gentry living in the NE of Scotland founded the Club in 1777. The founder members, as taken from the original documents listed on their website, in 1777 (with some interpretation) were:

	additional members listed 1778
Alexander J Threiben	William F Kirkham
John J Platigo	William C Airlie
Robert D Saffree	James F Arthur
Alexander J Valbere (Holburn)	Alexander C Boucheure
William J Memrie	Alexander F Sullivan
Louis J Inchmoore	Sir William Forbes GMM
Capt. James Philbroth	
Alexander O Aicheson	
Alexander H Troup	
Thomas McCleod	
John Dalrymple	
Thomas Pomfry	
Robert S Broadland	

The original course of 9-holes was played on the *public commonty* (Fraserburgh Links) but due to congestion and danger to the public, was moved to Philorth Links in 1891, thanks to the generosity of Alexander Fraser, the 17th Lord Saltoun. Lord Saltoun was the Grand Master Mason of Scotland from 1897–1900.

Their first Captain was John Reiach who was a Banker. G M Joss won the first scratch medal and R Mutch the handicap trophy. Lieutenant Gairdner RN presented a *Brass Cleek* to be competed for by the members and Lord Saltoun presented three medals to be played for in competition: gold, silver and bronze.

Thereafter the membership is recorded as follows:

Hon. Captain	Lord Saltoun
Captain	Thomas Park
Vice-Captain	Rev. GW Stewart
Vice-Captain Secretary	Rev. GW Stewart
and Treasurer	David Bruce
Council members:	James Milne, GM Joss, George Stephen, William Noble and William Grant.
Other members:	James Mitchell (Fisherman) Mr Canna (Harbour Treasurer)

1780 Society of Golfers at Aberdeen,

Wealthy merchants and businessmen instituted the Society in 1783. It most probably existed before 1783, as the ballot box, which is still in possession of the club, bears the inscription, 'The Aberdeen Golf Club 1780'. The Club had uniforms and no doubt wined and dined, but all records prior to 1815 have been lost!

It was reconstituted as the Royal Aberdeen Golf Club, Balgownie, in 1810. They initially played over the Queen's Links, behind Aberdeen's football stadium and continued to play over those Links and Broad Hill until 1888, when under the leadership of Captain H V Brooke, they moved to their present location of Balgownie, Bridge of Don, on the opposite side of the River Don. It is now known as the Royal Aberdeen Golf Club.

The new course was designed by Archie and Robert Simpson and has been upgraded in length and re-bunkered by James Braid to its present layout.

1786 Crail Golfing Society

Crail Golfing Society was founded in February 1786 by 11 gentlemen at a meeting held in the *Golf Inn*, which became their favoured meeting place for dining after golf. Members being fined for non-attendance, usually an additional munchkin of punch.

Official uniforms had to be worn at the dinners, comprising red jackets with yellow buttons. There was a similar fine for being improperly dressed. The 11 founder members were:

> Sir Charles Erskine, Bart.
> Methven Erskine
> David Erskine
> William Erskine
> Capt. Charles Ranken
> John Chiene, CB
> George Chiene

William Chiene
Patrick Murray
David Moncur
Daniel Conolly

Capt. Charles Ranken was the first Captain of the Society, Patrick Murray was their Chaplain and Daniel Conolly was the landlord of the *Golf Inn*. The first secretary, Stuart Grace, was not admitted to the Society until a week later in March.

Grace was at that time also the secretary of the R&A. Later Sir Charles, Thomas and Methven Erskine were all raised to a peerage becoming the 8th, 9th and 10th Earls of Kellie.

The founder members were landowners, Naval and Army Officers, a Writer to the Signet, ship masters, farm tenants, baillies of Crail and the landlord of the local inn.

The club was dissolved in 1813 and not revived until the end of 19th century.

The Society initially played their golf on an East Fife promontory known as Fife Ness. The 18-hole course, which was designed by Old Tom Morris in 1895, was and is still known as the Balcomie Links. A modern course has since been designed by Gil Hanse, alongside the former and is known as Craighead; both being operated by Crail Golf Club.

1787 Earlsferry Golf Society

The foundation of the Society was first recorded in 1787, at a meeting convened by the then Captain (unknown) to be held on the 1 May advertising the occasion in the *Caledonian Mercury* with dinner to follow.

This would suggest that the membership was numerous and of well-to-do individuals. The secretary, Patrick Plenderleath, who was a Writer of the Signet, signed the notice. Plenderleath's father was the Factor to Sir John Anstruther of Anstruther, who lived in Elie House.

In 1812, the tenant ploughed up the land used for the course and the Society ceased to exist. It was resurrected in 1832 under the name of Earlsferry Abbey Golf Society. That year their first silver medal was won by George Wood of Colinburgh, subsequently, John Swayne of Elie won it the next year.

A third version of the club was formed in 1858 and was entitled the Earlsferry and Elie Golf Club. This was disbanded in 1912 to be succeeded by the Golf House Club, Elie, which had been established in 1875 on land adjacent to the former with its own clubhouse.

In the same year, 1875, the Earlsferry Thistle Golf Club was formed, which was predominantly an artisan club. One of its early members was James Braid, who was born in Earlsferry in 1870.

1787 Glasgow Golf Club

22 wealthy merchants and army officers founded the Club in 1787, although a minute exists referring to golf facilities on Glasgow Green dated 1760. It is recorded in Kevin McGhee's article 'Anent the Golf—' that, *the competitors to the initial silver club competition are nevertheless listed as the founder members. Some of whom were of a military background, they are:*

Major Archibald Campbell, later an MP, who won the competition, Captain Thomas Peters, Captain David Shanks and William Bogle Junior, who became a Lieutenant-Colonel before being killed in the Napoleonic Wars. The remainder included, John and George Hamilton, James Black and Laurence Craigie, who were merchants in the city trading in sugar and rum.

Many were members of the West India Club and the Sugar Association. Six belonged to The Pig Club, five to The Hodge Podge Club and others to the Board of Green Cloth. Most were described as being of Glasgow's bluest blood. Three, James Black, Laurence Craigie and John Hamilton became the Lord Provost of Glasgow.

Two were members of the Lodge of Glasgow St John and at least seven were members of the Glasgow Kilwinning Lodge No. 4, sadly no records existed between 1775 and 1808, to verify there were more than seven. Others may have been members of the Glasgow Argyle Lodge, but its records have also been lost.

They played over Glasgow Green until 1794 when they ceased due largely to many of their members being called away to serve their country in the Napoleonic Wars. The Club recommenced in 1809 until 1835 when it ceased to be played over the Green due to municipal drainage works.

In 1870, the Club started to expand, initially to Queens Park, then after four years to Alexandra Park and in 1895 to Blackhill, before the current course at Killermont was secured for private play. Old Tom Morris designed this course in 1904.

During this period the Club also opened another course at Irvine in Ayrshire, (Glasgow) Gailes Links; this course being designed by Willie Park Jnr. in 1912.

1791 Burntisland Golf Club

It is recorded in 1791 that, A golfing club was instituted lately by the gentlemen of the town and neighbourhood, although the club accepts 1797 as their date of inception. Burntisland Golf House Club, which was founded in 1898, has its origins in the Burntisland Golf Club.

They first played their golf on links at the east end of Dodhead High Street on a course of 15-holes, but the links became too congested, so the course was moved to the north-east of the town.

The new course was initially only 6-holes but was later extended to a full 18-holes that were designed by Willie Park Jnr. in 1898. James Braid redesigned it in 1922.

The former links are now used as a public park and the only connection to its past is a crazy green and the Golf Tavern pub, where presumably the founders originally dined after play.

1791 Cruden Bay Golfing Society

The Society was formed in 1791 and played on open links over Ward Hill near Slains Castle in the older part of Cruden Bay. There is evidence that golf was still being played there in 1883.

When the railways came in the late 19th century, the Great North of Scotland Railway Company (GNSR) laid out the Cruden Bay golf course on a new site, designed by Old Tom Morris and assisted by Archie Simpson; it opened in 1899.

The new club gave extended playing privileges to local residents, who were called the Port Erroll Golf Club.

The course was redesigned by Tom Simpson and Herbert Fowler in 1926, although the positions of the greens remained unaltered.

1793 Kingsbarns Golfing Society

Kingsbarns Golfing Society was formed in 1793 by gentlemen who played over the links of Kingsbarns prior to dining in the *Golf Hall*. They wined and dined and wagered in the Hall until 1850 when the tenant farmer of the Combo Estate ploughed up the links for arable use; this being considered a more profitable use of the land.

After being prompted and encouraged by Lady Erskine of Combo, the Society was re-established in 1922 as the Kingsbarns Golf Club. The 9-hole course, laid out by Willie Auchterlonie, served the locals until the onset of the Second World War when the links were mined for national security and not restored after the war for another 55 years.

Golf was resurrected on the links at the beginning of the 21st century with a new 18-hole layout, designed by Kyle Philips, which is now used as a Championship venue.

1793 Fortrose Golf Society

There is recorded evidence of golf having been played over Chanonry (now Fortrose) in 1702 but it was not until 1793 that its existence was firmly established. A notice was published in the *Caledonian Mercury, on* 27 June 1793, calling for members to attend an Annual General Meeting of the Society on the 1 July in Williamson's Tavern.

Dinner was to commence at 4 pm and no doubt golf would have been a precursor to this event. There were two officers of the Society named in the notice, Charles Mackenzie, the President, and Duncan Munro, the croupier.

A croupier in these early days would either have been the vice-chairman or, more likely, the member who managed the betting, this being a central part of golf club dinners during this early period.

The Mackenzie family owned the village of Fortrose, which was later sold to the Rosehaugh Estate. Charles Mackenzie was the elder son of Colin Mackenzie, the 6th Laird of Kilroy, and became the 7th Laird in 1858 on the death of his father. Their son, Colin, became a Baronet in 1836.

At the time of the AGM, Charles was listed as an ensign to the 78th Regiment of Foot, in which his younger brother Alexander was the Lieutenant-Colonel. Alexander was also a golfer and had a distinguished career in the military and as a member of parliament for both Cromarty and Ross-shire in successive parliaments.

Duncan Munro of Culcairn was also a military man and was Captain Lieutenant in the 78th Highland Regiment and aide-de-camp to Lt. Col. Alexander Mackenzie. He later served in India and on his return was made Lieutenant-Colonel of the Wester Ross Regiment.

Other early members of the Society who are recorded as playing over the links at the end of the 18th century are: the local minister the Rev. Wood, Dr Tulloch, the local doctor, and Mr John MacQueen, the Rector of Fortrose Academy.

The initial course was laid out over the Chanonry Ness promontory part which is now included in the present layout. The society ceased to exist around the end of the 18th century due to the Napoleonic Wars in Europe, which created economic turmoil and demographic change.

This left a large time gap between the cessation of the original Society and the establishment of the new Fortrose and Rosemarkie Golf Club in 1888, which was founded by 17 members. Their first Captain was Alexander Mackenzie, Laird of Avoch, who was the son of Sir Alexander Mackenzie, the pioneer and explorer.

He remained their Captain for the next six years until his death in 1894. Alexander Mackenzie was also the first Captain of the London Scottish Golf Club at Wimbledon.

Other early members of the golf club included: three generals, members of the clergy, the provost, two billies, the town clerk, a sheriff and a local member of parliament. The clubhouse was sponsored and opened by Miss Mackenzie of Flowerburn in 1895.

1794 Dunbar Golfing Society

The first golfing organisation was recorded when a body known as the Dunbar Golfing Society set down its rules and listed 27 gentlemen founder members with play over the West Barns Links. A framed copy of the rules drawn up for the Society is displayed in the current clubhouse of Dunbar Golf Club. They were as follows:

1. The members shall meet at the West Barns Links on the second Wednesday of every month.
2. When the expense of each member for dinner amounts to 2 shillings and 6 pence, the club shall be dissolved.

3. Every member for every time he is absent shall pay 1 shilling towards defraying the expense of dinner.

Defraying the expense of dinner if absent was the usual custom among freemasons.

The playing of golf gradually disappeared from these links following the Napoleonic Wars (1794–1815) for thereafter they became a rifle range. This ceased when the West Barn Links were taken over for Napoleonic military training and exercises.

It was not until 1856 that six gentlemen formed Dunbar Golf Club at a meeting held in the town hall. The first Captain was a military man, George Warrender of Lochard, and John Jaffry took the minutes. George Warrender later became the 6th Baronet of Bruntsfield.

The other five were Captain James Cox of the Berwickshire Militia, Lieutenant John Stewart, William Anderson, James Brand and John Jaffry. At the time, Dunbar was a military town and the military services played an important part in the creation and running of the club.

Golf was now played over the East Barns Links, which was known as Broxmouth Links. The course was later redesigned five times before it finally became the course that is known today.

The Duke and Duchess of Roxburghe provided the club with their first clubhouse in 1871, however, this was superseded by a new clubhouse in 1902 that is still in use today having been extended in 1968.

1810 Montrose Golf Club

William Coull in his book 'Golf in Montrose' states that, *Royal Montrose is considered to be the 9th oldest golf club in the world and one of the very few to have been in continuous existence and still playing on the same links, but according to other records it is the 12th oldest, excluding golf societies.*

Montrose Golf Club was first set up in 1810 by golfers determined to protect their links for future generations. This encouraged the creation of many different golf clubs playing over the same ground.

They originally played on the East Links until the town council decided at the end of the 19th century that they wished to preserve this area of the links for leisure and commercial development. At the time there were many clubs playing golf over these links and the action of the town council forced them to relocate to the north and east.

Fortunately, the area of the links was extensive and there were no problems accommodating them in their new locations. Three clubs survived up until the end of 2019, Royal Montrose, Montrose Caledonia and Montrose Mercantile, however, following a recent merger in 2020, there are now just two remaining.

There is evidence of golf being played over these links since 1562, although it was not until 1810 that a formalised golf club was created. Harry Colt recreated the original 1562 layout in 1913. He also designed the adjacent Broomfield course in 1907, both of which are still in play.

Although the foundation date of Montrose Golf Club is 1810, this is only defined by the date on the embossed cover of the first minute book. The first minutes available are dated from 1813 and the first recorded Captain of the Club was James Bertram in 1817.

The Royal Montrose Mercantile Golf Club is a product of the original Montrose Golf Club founded in 1810, that was bestowed Royal Patronage in 1845 by Prince Albert, the husband of Queen Victoria. This allowed the name to be changed to the Montrose Royal Albert Golf Club.

In 1986, the Club merged with Montrose Victoria Golf Club, founded in 1864, to form the Royal Montrose Golf Club. However, on 1 November 2019, Royal Montrose and Montrose Mercantile, founded in 1879, merged to form the Royal Montrose Mercantile Golf Club. The merged club has its base in the Royal Montrose clubhouse.

There have been several Montrose clubhouses over the years, but initially, they played without one, no doubt meeting and dining in a local tavern. It was not until 1866 that they had their first clubhouse, a domestic property named *Southfield*, which they rented until 1890; it overlooks the present 18th green.

William Coull's 'Golf in Montrose' states, *There is a school of thought that a strong masonic thread ran through the organisation and rituals of early golf clubs. These point to the importance of dining and conviviality among friends, club uniforms, ceremonies, toasts, exclusion of women and the use of the* black ball *to control membership. These were all part of the early Montrose Golf Club and of others.*

The dates of the earliest 17 clubs and societies above relate to the first recorded meeting date, but it is likely that 18th century Scottish societies had been meeting well before the dates recorded.

In the early days, the social activities of wining, dining and betting were as important as golf. The social club as a concept has been around since 1620 and social clubs since 1640. The term *golf club* did not exist so it was a small step to combine social activities with golf and thereby create a golf club or golf society.

The use of a black ball for membership of golf clubs is also based on a masonic tradition, as one such club describes:

When a person wished to join the club, he was selected by each member placing a white or black ball into the Yes or No compartments of a wooden box, which was vintage masonic practice. The candidate had to receive a two-thirds majority to be accepted.

In 1864 this was reduced to one black, (which) was enough for the individual to be refused membership. No reason was given to the unsuccessful candidate, and nobody knew who had blackballed him.

The use of the black ball is a precursor of the *secret ballot*.

Coull continues, *gentlemen, officers of the military, and members of the professional class were the predominant members of early golf clubs. Members of early Freemasonry came from the same background. So, in those early years, it is not unreasonable to deduce that the influence they had on each other would have been significant.*

Consequently, when the gutta-percha ball came in, golf became more affordable and some golf clubs, such as Montrose, split up and formed offshoots, i.e. the Royal Albert Golf Club was for the original members and the Victoria Golf

Club consisted principally of the newer golfers, who were traders.

In the 19th century, golf began to expand exponentially with the introduction of the gutta-percha ball in 1848 which cost only a fraction of a feathery. Golf was now to become an occupation of the middle class and no longer be reliant on the privileged few.

In 1866, there were 38 golf clubs listed playing on 23 courses, but by 1888, this had risen to 197 and 126, respectively.

David Stirk further suggests in his book 'Golf—the History of an Obsession' that, *Golf like colf* (an early Dutch game played on ice) *could well have died out in the early 18th century but for the freemasons.*

The game was developed and sustained by their enthusiasm during the period of 1750 to 1850 for only members of the aristocracy and wealthy gentlemen could afford to play golf in the early years, as the cost of featheries was expensive.

However, this changed in the 19th century when the gutta-percha ball was introduced, which brought the game into the realm of the middle classes.

It was thought that the sudden expansion of golf clubs during the latter part of the 19th century was due to the coming of the railways. However, Michael Morrison in his book entitled' The Great English Golf Boom 1864–1914' Identifies that the invention of the bicycle was the prime influence. The invention of the railways occurred earlier in the century.

During the 17th and 18th centuries, both Freemasonry and golf developed along parallel lines and in similar locations. The gentlemen involved were often the same largely due to the social circles which they frequented.

Golf during this period was a pastime of the wealthy and Freemasonry was a vehicle for the hierarchy. It will also be noted that many of the founder members were also of a military background.

Chapter Four
Early Military Field Lodges

It became clear during this research that many founder members of early golf clubs had a military rank or background. This led to an investigation into the possibility of a connection between early military lodges and the establishment of golf clubs.

During the 16th century, most of the conflicts were fought by unregulated armies raised by various factions including Oliver Cromwell and members of the aristocracy. When Cromwell discharged the monarchy and England became a republic, he created an army for his protection.

This army, however, was disbanded in 1660 by Charles II when the monarchy was restored, except for one household brigade, which is now the Coldstream Guards. Subsequently in 1661, Charles II issued a royal warrant creating the first regiments of the British Army.

The first military field lodges were not established until nearly a century later. Thus, during the 18th century, a considerable number of military lodges came into existence, initially all under the Irish Constitution, possessing the right to meet legally at whatever place the regiment might find itself.

The first such Lodge was founded in 1732 at Bray in Co. Wicklow by the 1st Battalion of the Royal Scots. Scotland had its first military lodge in 1743, the 55th Regiment of Foot, which was disbanded in 1748; whilst the first English regimental lodge was founded in 1747, the Duke of Norfolk's Regiment of Foot.

Subsequently, travelling warrants were issued by the Grand Lodges of Ireland, Scotland, England (Antients and Moderns), France and the United States of America.

Research into the British Military Masonic Field Lodges of the Regiments of Foot during the period of 1743 to 1850, established that the earliest formation date was 1747 and all bar one of the lodges were disbanded by 1864. Permanent regimental lodges were formed at a subsequent period.

The regiments themselves were dispersed over the world during this period with only a few times being garrisoned in the UK. The dates have been traced when this occurred in Scotland, England and Ireland, and related to the dates of the foundation of various golf clubs in these countries.

A match was found with five Scottish clubs, two of which were golfing societies, see below, and two in Ireland, see Chapter Eight.

They are:

Bruntsfield Links Golfing Society founded 1761

The *64th Regiment of Foot (2nd Staffordshire)* was garrisoned in Scotland 1760–1763. Their colonel was General Hon. George Cary.

Crail Golfing Society founded 1786

The *56th Regiment of Foot (West Essex)* was garrisoned in

Scotland 1784–1788. Their colonel was General Hunt Walsh.

Glasgow GC founded 1787

The *56th Regiment of Foot (West Essex)* was garrisoned in Scotland 1784–1788. Their colonel was General Hunt Walsh.

North Berwick GC founded 1832

The *1st Regiment of Foot (Royal Scots)* was garrisoned in Scotland 1830. Their colonel was General Gordon, 5th Duke of Gordon, who was also the Grand Master Mason of Scotland in 1792–1794.

Leven Club founded in 1846

The *1st Regiment of Foot (Royal Scots)* was garrisoned in Scotland in 1846. Their colonel was Sir James Kempt.

Enquiries were made of these societies and golf clubs to establish if any of the above colonels in chief were founder members, but none have been matched. Further enquiries were also made to ascertain the exact location of their garrisons on the above dates.

A schedule of overseas postings of the various regiments is listed in the appendices. Sadly, it has not yet been possible to establish the exact location of their garrisons in England and Scotland, the military records of these postings are not in the general domain.

The research produced a potted history of all Regiments of Foot that received a warrant to form a military lodge up until 1860.

These include the 1st (Royal), 4th (the King's Own), 12th (East Suffolk), 17th (Leicestershire), 22nd (Cheshire), 23rd (Royal Welsh Fusiliers), 31st (Huntingdonshire), 32nd (Cornwall), 42nd (the Royal Highland), 43rd (Monmouthshire), 51st (8th Marines), 56th (West Essex), 64th (2nd Staffordshire), 70th (Surrey), 71st (Highland), 80th (Light Armed), 94th (Royal Welsh Volunteers), Royal Scots Greys, Royal Scots Fusiliers, Durham Militia and the Forfar & Kincardine Militia.

These field lodges are listed in the appendices which contains a brief history of the development of each regiment's field lodge and likewise the postings of regiments with lodges prior to 1860.

It would appear from this research that there is little direct connection between the military field lodges and the foundation of golf clubs.

Furthermore, there is no match with any of the overseas golf clubs other than Bray in Ireland, although it is possible the foundation of Charleston GC, South Carolina and Savannah GC, Georgia, may have been influenced by the British Military, as a result of their occupation.

However, it is quite clear that the brotherly bond established by Freemasonry would have been and still is an essential requirement of any fighting force.

The research conducted during the compilation of this book and of others leaves little doubt that many early military officers were associated with and played an active role in the establishment of early golf clubs and golf societies, i.e., General Alexander MacKay would have served at Bray in Ireland, likewise Colonel James Pringle.

Chapter Eleven, throws further light on the role that the military played in the dissemination of Freemasonry and golf around the globe. The evidence gleaned to date, as to whether that was responsible for the foundation of golf clubs overseas can only be conjecture.

However, the military's establishment of colonial masonic lodges cannot be denied and led to the proliferation of Freemasonry around the globe.

Chapter Five
Social Strata in the Late 18th and 19th Century

The stage had been set for regular social interaction by the early golfers prior to the formation of clubs and societies. Their development to the club structure of today was evolving slowly, many starting as golf societies before they became established as golf clubs.

One such golfing society was founded in 1774, Musselburgh Golf Club, although their records did not start until 1784. Nevertheless, the Club has a silver cup that bears testimony to previous annual winners. It was the custom with contemporary societies for the winner of the cup to be declared captain of the society for the ensuing year.

Thomas McMillan, who won the inaugural event, presented the Silver Cup to the Club. There is no mention of a uniform, but a bets book was kept. The first minute dated 1784 refers to them as the Company of Golfers and it was not until 1786 that they regularly referred to themselves as a club.

It was recorded in the minutes in 1788 that, *they dined and wined well and that everyone must pay his share;* a prerequisite of Freemasonry.

Scottish Golf History states that during the 18th century when the early golf clubs were formed, the status of being a freemason or a Burgess was a condition of entry in both Scotland and England. At least one golf historian has eluded freemasons established many of the early Scottish golf clubs.

The same may have applied to England as the Royal Blackheath Golf Club was only open to freemasons until 1789 and for a generation thereafter there was a clique of freemasons called the Knuckle Club who played out of season on Blackheath to avoid non-masonic members.

Alastair and James Johnston state in their book, 'The Chronicles of Golf 1457–1857', that, *The influence of freemasons in the evolution of early golfing societies should be recognised but not overstated. Undoubtedly, many of the policies practised by freemasons would have been incorporated into the rules and protocol of the golfing societies.*

There is no question that many characteristics, such as the obligation to dine after golf, the requirements to swear oaths of allegiance and (to) wear society uniforms, as well as the other ceremonial trappings, seem to have been borrowed from the mysteries associated with Freemasonry.

They further state, *We think it quite likely that the Leith and Blackheath Societies were closely associated with the freemason movement. On the other hand, the less eminent clubs, which were founded in the late 18th century outside the primary metropolitan areas of Scotland, appear to have been launched by the genuine aspiration to enjoy competitive golf in a more regulated environment, rather than being motivated by a more obscure, mystical agenda.*

This was further elaborated on by Dr Wade Cormack in his article entitled 'History of Golf in Northern Scotland 1600–1800' where he explores the associational culture in relation to golf.

His overview is that, *Prior to the late–18th century in Northern Scotland people played golf at school or had informal gatherings. Cromarty had regular golf meetings in the 1750s comprising a group of friends who were all from the professional class and local elites who enjoyed golf on the links followed by hospitality given by one of their most prominent members, William Forsyth. These informal gatherings were vibrant and well-organised.*

He further postulates that, *The creation of sporting clubs was part of a larger cultural trend known as associational culture. This was largely an urban phenomenon with its roots tracing back to the aftermath of the English Civil War. It facilitated the widespread creation of voluntary associations, which contemporary members named clubs, societies, companies, academies or fraternities (Freemasonry).*

Voluntary associations were founded upon ideas of leisure, philanthropy, philosophy, rationalism, self-improvement and sociability, and were a quintessential part of polite society.

At club meetings gentlemen, and occasionally their wives, socialised, built friendships, solidified alliances and strengthened family bonds. Moreover, clubs and societies attracted wealthy patrons; it was a sign of wealth and status to be able to participate in this section of polite society.

His article records that there were three such golf clubs in Northern Scotland, namely: Fraserburgh Golf Club (1777); the Society for Golfers in Aberdeen (1780); and the Fortrose Golfing Society (1793). It is understood that these clubs normally gathered monthly for golf, which was followed by a meal at a local establishment.

There is no doubt that the social life in the British Isles during the 18th century began to take on a substantially different individual character. From the time that Queen Anne came to the throne in 1702 until the day that George III died in 1820, government by the people had gradually become an established fact.

The change in the administration of the country reflected itself both in the classes and the masses, as well as in all kinds of institutions and customs.

This saw the development and growth of several important additions to daily life. One of the more influential aspects was the increase in periodical literature. Another was the production of shows of every imaginable kind, such as cock-fighting; some of these being geared to the masses.

These shows and other influential aspects increased the level of gambling for all classes, which for many was their downfall.

Every period has its essential characteristic and that of the 18th century is one of contrast. The substantial difference between the wealthy and the masses was prevalent at the beginning but, with the growth of the middle class, the importance of the hierarchy was gradually dumbed down.

It has already been established that golf in its early years was played by the aristocracy, the gentry, military officers and the professional classes. It is, therefore, necessary to look at the social structure that pervaded Britain at that formative period.

The Industrial Revolution was beginning to take off and society was developing a more socially active middle class. This led to many changes in the social order that permeated its way into all walks of life including the golf club.

In this respect, the uniform adopted by the early golfers was a necessity in many of the early clubs dictated by the social strata attached to those early golfers.

Bobby Burt in his article 'When Dressing for Golf Required Uniformity' gives an insight into the social strata in golf.

He states that, *The concept of the golfer's uniform started in Scotland and was derived from the Royal Company of Archers, who in December 1713 received a Royal Charter to be the sovereign's bodyguard.*

Comprised of Lords, Nobles and Gentlemen from the upper echelons of Edinburgh Society, they practised their archery skills and held archery competitions at Leith Links.

On the 14 June 1714, dressed in green military uniform with a feathered cap, some fifty members of the Royal Company of Archers, equipped in military array and distinguished by their proper standards, marched from Edinburgh to Leith for their first competition for the Silver Arrow.

Other units of soldiers or guards encountered on the way turned out to acknowledge this senior unit with a full military salute appropriate to the sovereign's forces. Subsequently, whenever the archers went to Leith Links for practise or competition the same honours were repeated, until archery at

Leith Links was prohibited in 1734 and archery practise was moved to the Meadows in Edinburgh.

Many of the Archers were also golfers who, after archery practise, would stay in Leith for a meal and play golf on the links, before returning to Edinburgh.

In this context, it is worth recording that in 1744, the surgeon John Rattray, who won golf's first competition for the silver club at Leith, pulled off a double triumph by also winning the Archer's Silver Arrow competition, held later the same year in Edinburgh.

Rattray went on to win the silver club again in 1745, but the Archer's records show no winner of the Silver Arrow for that year, possibly because they were all engaged elsewhere! (The Battle of Culloden?).

The military uniform of the Archers would not permit the free movement required for playing golf and so was less than ideal, whilst damage or soiling of the uniforms would be unacceptable.

Following lunch at one of the nearby local inns, usually Straiton's or Luckie Clephane's, golf matches would be made and played, followed by an evening meal before heading back to Edinburgh. Clothing worn for golf would be stored by the innkeeper along with clubs and a room was set aside for the participants to change, as required.

David Hamilton, in his book 'Golf—Scotland's Game', expands on the appearance of golfing uniforms by several clubs in the late 1700s, noting that, the uniforms, whilst unique to each club, were all in a style that was unmistakably military.

He writes, *In 1771, the Honourable Company of Edinburgh resolved to have their present Captain's picture in full length in his golfing dress and requested him to sit for the same. This was the portrait of William St Clair of Roslyn.*

He was dressed in a round blue Kilmarnock bonnet and a red coat cut after the fashion of the day; the knee breeches and stocking forming no part of the uniform.

Other clubs soon followed suit. In a minute dated 2 July 1790, the Burgess Golfing Society (now the Royal Burgess Golfing Society of Edinburgh) it was noted, members to wear an uniform as is universally done by other societies of golfers. The uniform for this Society was a scarlet jacket, black neck and badge, similar to the Royal Blackheath. (See 'The Chronicle of the Royal Burgess', by J C Robbie, 1936).

The R&A had red jackets with gold buttons and *two other golf clubs near neighbours of the R&A also had uniforms; Crail in 1792 had a scarlet jacket with plain yellow buttons whilst Kingsbarns chose a blue jacket.*

On the west coast of Scotland, the Glasgow Golf Club chose a grey jacket, which followed the lines of the old archery clubs and the exclusive social tone of the players.

R Browning notes that the Innerleven Golfing Society had the Prince Charles Tartan as part of their uniform, whilst Aberdeen Golf Club had two uniforms, red jackets to be worn whilst playing on the golf course and equally resplendent blue jackets to be worn whilst dining.

Wimbledon Park and London Scottish wore crimson jackets, primarily to give a warning to the public of their presence, as they played their golf on common land.

Hamilton continues, *Penalties were enforced for not wearing the appropriate uniform and a minute from a meeting held at Leith on 16 November 1787 stated that Lieutenant James Dalrymple of the 43rd Regiment was fined six pints for playing at five different times without his uniform.*

A minute of a meeting held on the following day states that, a uniform for the golfer was presented by Captain Lord Elcho and his council.

Uniforms for golf started to disappear in the middle of the 19th century as they became too expensive and restrictive to the golf swing.

Hamilton records that many of the older golf clubs continued to honour the tradition of wearing a coloured jacket. These are worn by the captain and past captains at all formal club functions such as the annual dinner, dinner with visiting clubs, or when invited to another club as a guest.

The short-style jacket maintains its military derivation, resembling the full-dress evening wear of senior military officers attending regimental functions.

The social economic structure of the late 18th century was about to change with the beginning of the Industrial Revolution and the advent of a people's democracy. This is further explained in the history of 'The Lodge of Good Report No 136 and its Meeting Places' by H R Sharp.

In this, he records that during this period, King George III (1738–1820) was monarch from 1760 to 1820, but 5 years after becoming king, he became unpopular and suffered vilification in the press.

At that time Britain had severe financial difficulties that were exacerbated by the cost of the Seven Years' War, which the king and his ministers had failed to address successfully. There was also political instability, which only improved after William Pitt the Elder became Prime Minister in 1766. It was during this period of unrest that the early lodges were founded.

Sharp's history states that, *The First Industrial Revolution took place in Britain between 1760 and 1830, powered by steam, laying the foundation for British wealth and power during the 19th century. It was during this period that Britain's American colonies won their independence under the 1783 'Treaty of Paris'.*

William Pitt the Younger became Prime Minister in 1783 and his first period in office continued until 1801. During this period the reign of George III continued but by 1788 his alleged madness caused the Regency Crisis. A Bill was proposed in 1789, which gave his eldest son, Prince George (Grand Master of England in 1790–1813), the right to act during his father's incapacity.

(However,) the King recovered his faculties and the Regency Bill was not enacted. In 1789, turmoil was created in Europe when the French Revolution erupted. This eventually led to a war that spread around the globe.

Sharp continues, *The late 1790s were troublesome for Freemasonry. Severely shaken by the French Revolution, rebellion in Ireland and working-class protests at home, the government of William Pitt the Younger feared a home-grown revolution.*

The administration had some reason to suspect radical societies, such as the London Corresponding Society and United Irish, of sedition. The members of these societies were sworn to secrecy, so the government proposed legislation banning meetings of any group requiring members to take an oath or obligation.

The new Act was called the *'Unlawful Societies Act'*, which would have destroyed Freemasonry. It was this '*Unlawful Societies Act of 1799*' that saw the first statute *for the more effectual suppression of societies established for seditious and treasonable purposes*; once enacted it affected all societies whose members were required to take an oath that was unauthorised by law and as such would thus be deemed *unlawful combinations*.

In consequence, the intervention by the Grand Master of the Antients, the 4th Duke of Atholl, and the Acting Grand Master of the Moderns, the Earl of Moira, was made, and they called a meeting with the Prime Minister, William Pitt, on 2 May 1799 to save the *Craft*.

This resulted in a special exempting clause being inserted into this legislation in favour of societies 'held under the Denomination of Lodges of Freemasons' provided that they had been *usually held before the Act*, and the places and times of meeting and the names, professions, age and addresses of the members were annually registered with the local Clerk to the Justices of the Peace.

Only lodges existing before the Act became law received its protection, consequently, to avoid this difficulty, both Grand Lodges began to reissue to new lodges the warrants of lodges that had become defunct before 12 July 1799. The Act remained in force until 1967 when this Act was repealed by a section of the *'Criminal Justice Act'*, which meant that the annual returns of all the lodges to the authorities ceased.

John Harris in his article concerning this Act stated, *freemasons being fearful of falling prey to this Act, as well as many Scottish lodges, burned or destroyed their priceless records. The Act did not specifically cite freemasons as being unlawful, but the mere threat was enough for many lodges to destroy evidence of their existence. At that time, some lodges had been in existence since c1600, which meant that 200 years of records were lost.*

Since 1997, several members of the British Government have attempted to pass laws requiring freemasons, who join the police or judiciary, to declare their membership publicly to the government amid accusations of freemasons performing acts of mutual advancement and favour-swapping.

This movement was led by Jack Straw, who was the Home Secretary from 1997 until 2001. In 1999, the Welsh Assembly became the only body in the United Kingdom to place a legal requirement on membership declaration for freemasons. Currently, existing members of the police and judiciary in England are asked to voluntarily admit to being freemasons.

However, all first-time successful judiciary candidates must declare their Freemasonry status before appointment.

Conversely, new members of the police are not required to declare their status.

In 2004, Rhodri Morgan, the first minister of the Welsh Assembly, said that he blocked Gerard Elias' appointment to Counsel General because of his links to hunting and Freemasonry, although it was claimed by non-Labour politicians that the real reason was to have a Labour supporter, Malcolm Bishop, in the role.

The early recognition of golf and Freemasonry being a pastime of the more affluent is recorded by David Stirk in his book 'History and Tradition' where he elaborates, *the Royal Company of Archers was from the start very much a company for the noblest in the land, and its membership in 1703 was in effect a list of Scottish nobility and particularly those of Flemish origin, namely Seton, Erskine, Stuart, Annadale, Eglinton, Montgomerie, St Clair, etc.*

Their families were officers in the Scots Guard, a regiment that replaced the Royal Company of Archers, and all were associated with Freemasonry.

William St Clair was their president and had won the Silver Arrow; John Rattray was a member and had also won the Silver Arrow. Thomas Kincaid was a member and a prominent member of the HCEG, and likewise David Drummond.

The Scots Guard were known as a neo-Templar organisation but when they were the Royal Company of Archers they had many ranks within it, i.e., Lieutenant, Captain, Captain-General, Brigadier, etc.

But it is interesting to note that the term Captain-General is also the 3rd officer of a Knights Templar Commandery, thus confirming (suggesting*) a direct link to the Knights Templars.*

I have seen no documentary evidence of this but the fact that the same term is used by both suggests there may have been a direct link.

Stirk further asserts that the effect of the 1745 uprising led to the dramatic arrival in Scotland of a Stuart Pretender to the throne of a Hanoverian king, which aroused all the romantic, passionate and tendentious character of the Celts. But not all Scots supported it. In such a climate, the freemasons were similarly divided.

After the Battle of Culloden, they found themselves in a very dangerous situation. It therefore fell on George II's General, the Duke of Cumberland, to be totally ruthless in his determination to eliminate all Jacobites; the breath of suspicion was enough to lead to imprisonment, torture and death.

During the rising some Scottish families were split and served on opposing sides, one such family, namely the Boyd's, were also members of the same lodge, the Old Masonic Lodge of Falkirk.

In this instance, General William Boyd, the 4th Earl of Kilmarnock, and his son Charles fought for the Jacobites, whilst his other two sons, James and William fought on the side of the King.

This ended tragically when James, who was part of the Duke of Cumberland's army, captured his father, General William Boyd, who was taken to the Tower of London before being beheaded for treason.

Charles escaped to France via the Isle of Arran and returned to Slains Castle, Aberdeen, much later after the rebellion had been concluded, where he was reconciled with his brother James.

Prior to the uprising William Boyd Snr was the Grand Master Mason of Scotland 1742–1743, he was also a member of the R&A as were the youngest two brothers. James was a member of HCEG.

The Carnegie family were another golfing family that served on both sides of the rising. Sir James Carnegie Bt. served with the Duke of Cumberland's army whilst his brother fought for the Jacobite cause.

The recognition of a secret society, most of whose members were Jacobites, would have been enough to ensure imprisonment or death for all its members. The immediate reaction of freemasons was to destroy all records.

Therefore, it is conjectured by David Stirk that all early records of golfing societies prior to 1745 were destroyed or lost. This is no longer the accepted view, as some clubs maintained all their records from their formation and likewise masonic lodges.

Chapter Six
Early Golf Clubs and Societies and Their Association with Freemasonry

One golf club that started as a society in 1761 was the Bruntsfield Golf Club, which changed its name to a club in 1787. In 1790, the Club stated that it had been established for 30 years, giving it a founding date of 1761.

There is not much evidence in relation to its association with Freemasonry but in a minute dated 1801 it is recorded, *It is recommended to the treasurer to purchase a dozen caps and aprons…expense to be paid out of the admission fund*; aprons being a part of a freemason's uniform.

Pat Colledge in his 'History of Bruntsfield Links Golfing Society' states that, *It was in 1761 that the Bruntsfield Links Golfing Society was inaugurated, which is the 4th oldest golfing body in the world; the oldest being the Royal Burgess Golfing Society of Edinburgh (1735).*

The histories of these clubs are closely entwined, although the origin of each remains obscure. There are, however, a number of references to them being in existence at these dates. (For instance,) *in the 'Reminiscences of the old Bruntsfield*

Links Golf Club', by Aitchison & Lorimer (1902), it is recorded that, *A Centenary Dinner, at which the Lord Provost was the guest of honour, was held in the Freemasons Hall on 28 March 1861.*

At the dinner, it was further recorded that the Bruntsfield Society broke away from the Burgess Club at Bruntsfield due to strong feeling regarding the loyal toast. (see later)

Furthermore, Pat Colledge asserts that, *In the mid–18th century, when both the Burgess and the Bruntsfield Societies were established, two matters of national importance occurred in Scotland, namely the growth of Freemasonry and the Jacobite Rebellion of 1745.*

These two events are inexplicably linked and there are historians who claim that the 45 Rebellion had its roots in Freemasonry. A common factor between them being an obsession for secrecy, as it was on such an issue that lives and reputations could depend in the aftermath of the Battle of Culloden.

Many of the golfers who had a military background would have been called away to fight in the Rebellion.

In the case of the Royal Burgess Golf Society, there is evidence of a major masonic presence and, divided as the nation was, almost equally between Jacobites and the anti-Jacobites, there can be little doubt that a substantial Jacobite element also existed.

In such circumstances, it would not be surprising if the early records of this Society had been destroyed. This was the case with other clubs at the time with apparently one exception The Honourable Company of Edinburgh Golfers.

The Society's position, in the general confusion in Scottish society at the time, is not known and there are those who believed it was formed from Burgess members with Jacobite inclinations. Accordingly, it may not be unreasonable to place more than a little emphasis on the speech made by Mr Josiah Livingston, Captain of the Society, at the centenary dinner mentioned above. Here it was stated that the origin of the Society was due to political causes. Mr Livingston then continued:

A hundred years ago brings us to a period when the recollection of Prince Charlie was vivid in men's minds, and the memories of those who had perished in the disastrous rising of 1745 were still fresh. There was a section of the old Burgess Club whose sympathies were with the lost cause. It was a hateful thing to them to be called upon to drink to the health of the representatives of the powers that then were, through whose instrumentality of the blood of their relatives and friends had flowed on the battlefield of the scaffold. Association with those who gloried in the downfall of their fondest illusions was increasingly distasteful and, after bearing with it for some time, they at last withdrew and founded The Bruntsfield Links Golf Club or Association, as it was then called.

When asked for his authority for this statement by Mr Lorimer, one of the authors of 'The Reminiscences' who had been present at the dinner, Mr Livingston replied, with a twinkle in his eye, that it could be found in the minute books!

Sadly, the early minute books could not be found and subsequently, the later ones were destroyed or lost as well.

The question (that) therefore remains: Was the Society Jacobite in origin? Mr Lorimer states unequivocally that the Society was an offshoot of the Burgess but makes no further comment.

However, Mr Dale Concannon in his book *Golf—The Early Days* (1995) maintains that the Royal Burgess was joined in 1761 with the newly formed Bruntsfield Links Golfing Society, which was made up of loyal supporters of the exiled Bonnie Prince Charlie.

Concannon continues, *They established their own club because they had little wish to drink the health of King George of England. Little is known about the Scottish rebels that formed the first Bruntsfield Club, but they lived harmoniously with their colleagues at Royal Burgess for over two centuries, first at Bruntsfield itself and then, as the course became overcrowded, at Musselburgh after 1874.*

All the records of the Royal and Ancient Golf Club of St Andrews are intact from 1754. This is the year when the members subscribed for a silver club and the rules of golf were adopted. The competition for the trophy was initially *open* to anyone. This was later amended in 1766, as recorded in the 'Book of Record', which has the following resolution:

Wee (sic) the Nobleman and Gentlemen subscribing admirers of the ancient and very healthful exercise of golf, and at the same time having the interest and prosperity of the ancient city of St Andrews the alma mater of the golf heart.

Did this day agree to meet once every fortnight by 11 o'clock at the Golf House and to play a round of the links (in terms of the Regulations of the silver club); to dine together at Baillie Glass's and to pay each a shilling for his dinner—the absent as well as present.

This obligation (is) to be binding upon each of the subscribers during the six months following this date and for every summer hereafter, unless the subscribers shall give in a declinature to be sustained and recorded in this book.

The Captain and his Council finding that the Members of the Club had signed upon detached pieces of paper did and hereby do authorise and appoint their Clerk to affix their names as obligatory upon their persons to fulfil the promises.

The Society of St Andrews Golfers followed the usual traditions of other societies and early clubs and engaged in wining and dining of heroic proportions. They also had fines for non-attendance and wore uniforms. However, the wager book was not such a prominent feature. In 1834, they became the Royal and Ancient Golf Club of St Andrews.

Other masonic connections are listed as, Alexander Duncan, a known Master Mason, who became Captain of the R&A, after having been Captain of HCEG and Captain of Blackheath GC, and newspaper records of 1853.

These records indicate that when the new clubhouse was being constructed, a bottle was found containing two golf balls, copies of *The Times*, the *Fifeshire Journal* and the *Fife Herald*, together with various masonic items.

Another early club offered the following information. Old Manchester is a club without a course and Graham Waters, Old Manchester (Club), advised that whilst there is hearsay that Freemasonry was involved in the formation of the Club in 1818, there are no records currently available to give any further evidence.

Graham Waters was advised that several lodges were formed by the military whilst being stationed away from base and it appears that there were a number of Scottish regiments involved at the time of the Club's formation. In a note from their minute book of 1850, it was noted that Major Douglas of the 79th *Regiment* and General Reid came to dinner.

The founder members of Old Manchester are listed as: George Fraser, William Mitchell, Michael Harbottle, George Hole, Vernon Royal, Jonathon Andrew, James Burt, Daniel Brant and David Scott. They were all involved in the cotton trade but there is no record of them being freemasons.

A further interesting insight into early club structures is given to us by Leven GCs. Archie Shanks, who was the Club Captain, advised that to his knowledge Leven has no connection with the masonic movement, but outlined the structural make-up of the various Leven Golf Clubs. i.e., Innerleven GC (1820) would have been for the gentry and Leven GC (1847) for the white-collar workers.

These two merged in 1956 to form the Leven Golfing Society. Leven Thistle GC (1867) was for blue-collar workers and is still operating, sharing playing rights over the Leven Links.

Leven Golf Society also incorporates Leven Ladies GC (1891), which merged with the Society in 1963. There are several freemason lodges in the area, but as far as is known they have no particular connection with golf.

At Prestwick GC, founded in 1851, it is recorded in the club history that of the founding members, Major James Fairlie was the prime mover.

Their first Club Captain was Archibald Montgomerie, the 13th Earl of Eglinton; a well-known title in Freemasonry and served as a military officer under George Washington. The names of the early treasurers and secretaries were James Kennedy, John Cuthbert and W Kirkland.

However, Czeslaw Kruk advised that the Portobello Golf Club, founded in 1853, did have connections to Freemasonry. Many members of Portobello GC were also members of Portobello (Porty) Lodge No. 226. There are unfortunately no details of their masonic connection recorded in the Club's records.

The only reference from Czeslaw's book '155 Years of Golf in Portobello' is that George Smith was a member of that lodge and Captain of the Club in 1883 and 1902–05. He was also Captain of Royal Musselburgh GC in 1898. The one other named member recorded as being a freemason is R Murray in 1922.

J V Harris in his book 'Dunbar Golf' states that, *A small group of gentlemen calling themselves the Dunbar Golfing Society recorded their existence in 1794 as one of Scotland's ten oldest golf organisations.*

The proof of their existence is documented in The Haddingtonshire Courier 4 March 1881 written about the Regulations of the Dunbar Golfing Society, 14 May 1794.

The book then lists the signatures of 26 members including Charles Hay, Christopher Middlemass, John

Dudgeon and Charles Lorimer. The fact that Thomas Smith is cited as an absentee to the signing of the document suggests that the Society existed at an earlier date.

Harris continues, *At the time of Dunbar's (Golfing) Society there were almost no golf clubs, as we would recognise them today. The game might have better been called a pastime rather than a sport since societies were few and very small in size.*

The less wealthy contented themselves with hitting a ball on almost any bare ground available and virtually all golf was played for a wager in a singles format. The use of the word club in the second regulation is not proof that society had the permanence we associate with that expression today.

Similar golf organisations would often gather to play and compete at many different locations but be unlikely to afford a clubhouse. In the case of the Dunbar Society, (the) nearby Beltonford Inn (or the Hay Arms) could have served as a home.

At least 10 of the signatories plus the three specifically mentioned namely William Wightman—Doctor, Master of Masonic Lodge in 1802, James Lindsay—member of masonic lodge and A Fraser—member of a masonic lodge, have been identified as members of the masonic lodge of Dunbar Castle.

Clearly, the majority were men of standing and substance in the town. However, the link to the masonic tradition is worthy of investigation.

The early records of the Dunbar Castle Lodge, founded in 1758, are fragmentary and its authorised history, by Rev. J McMartin, contains no references to golf. It is generally accepted that the freemasons were at the heart of Scotland's early organised golf.

J V Harris further records in his book that golf historian, Geddes, stated: *These societies were very much the preserve of wealthy merchants, academics and professional men who saw golf as a means to display status, wealth and achievement. It was also socially exclusive, i.e. forbidding lady membership. The expensive nature of golf equipment would have reinforced this preserve.*

These brief histories of the golfing societies have similar characteristics; the most important of these was to dine after playing golf. They had club uniforms, ceremonies, fines in the form of drink for being absent or other offences and toasts including the masonic *three times three*.

When necessary new membership was controlled with the use of the *black ball*. The wearing of uniforms at dinner has a direct link with military conventions.

All the early societies had similar customs not related to golf, they shared a secret—again not related to golf—and that they were not formed with the primary object of playing golf. What was originally offered was a 'package deal' of golf, dinner and mysteries. Those who took up the offer had to be affluent and leading members of the community, i.e. nobles, gentlemen, military officers, advocates, bankers, flourishing tradesmen and the like. Freemasons were often to be seen in public, in ceremonial processions, wearing uniforms and regalia. The requirement for golfers to wear a uniform on the green had nothing to do with the wearing of a red jacket on public courses. The red jackets being a warning to members of the public sharing the same open space.

By 1800 there were seven golf societies, but during the course of the next 50 years, their number only increased by 10, including two in England. The tide had turned. Golf had become a more widely accessible and affordable game, particularly with the introduction of the gutty ball in the middle of the century.

In the early 19th century, there were only two clubs in England, Blackheath, 1608, and Manchester, 1819, but with the growth of the sport more clubs were being formed and the members of Blackheath had a strong influence on the following:

Westward Ho! (Royal North Devon GC),	1864
Royal Wimbledon GC,	1865
Hoylake (Royal Liverpool GC)	1869
Great Yarmouth GC,	1882
Royal St George's GC,	1887

Neil Scaife in his book, '400 Years of the Blackheath Golfer' he records that the *earliest written evidence of the existence of the Club is from a Golf Club cash book, dated 1787. The entry was headed Chocolate House Blackheath 7 April 1787—Rec'd of the following Gentlemen being Subscribers to the Golf Club for 1787.*

This is followed by the names of 55 members, nearly all of them Scottish, Highland and Lowland. The name of the treasurer was an Englishman named Charles Kensington.

Of the membership, at least 30 were merchants of London and 20 or more can be traced as having residences at Blackheath, nearly all on the west side of the heath where the

Green Man tavern, one of the earliest meeting places, was situated. 30 of the members were referred to as gentlemen of the London Scots Society in a newspaper article published in September 1787 reporting on last Saturday's game on the heath. (This is) a term that obliquely refers to the Blackheath Golfing Society.

The first name on the list was Captain, Coll Turner, followed by Secretary, Henry Callender, who became Captain in 1790, 1801 and 1807. Third name was William Innes who was born in Edinburgh and became a successful London merchant trading in the West Indies.

He was also a member of parliament for Ilchester 1774–1775. In his will, he bequeathed a silver club to the club, which was to be played for each year. After the play, they wined and dined in the tavern and arranged bets for the next games.

A Blackheath Golf Club Betts Book dated 1791 survives and provides a fascinating record of where and (on) what terms the early members played the game.

Scaife continues, *that 1789 saw the foundation of the Knuckle Club as a separate Winter Club whilst still acknowledging the Blackheath Club, which played in the summer, as its parent. It was a masonic lodge within the Blackheath Club and was set up with 22 regulations, including the initiation ceremony, and continued as a lodge until 1825, when it was wound up.*

The Knuckle Club was very similar to the early Scottish Golfing Societies with the obligation to dine after playing golf.

As previously recorded, *They adopted club uniforms, engaged in formal ceremonies, imposed fines for absence and other offences, and toasts were drunk, including the masonic three times three. New members were controlled by the use of the black ball.*

The above is a description of the Knuckle Club and is elaborated on as follows: All members were freemasons. They met after golf at a tavern called the Green Man. They played for a gold medal that was decorated with human knuckles and it was obligatory for anyone wishing to speak at the dinner to be holding a knucklebone in his hand.

New members went through an initiation ceremony and then underwent a severe examination before being passed the *sign* in style! There was a well-kept record of wagers.

The wining and dining were stupendous and members were fined for a breach of the rules, this often being a gallon of claret, which was to be drunk on the premises. There were many toasts drunk during the evening.

Neil Scaife continues, *There can be little doubt that the concept of playing golf before feasting was a largely masonic invention. Freemasons shared a secret, and after a time, they began to play golf with non-masons, who were not admitted to their mysteries.*

It is notable that all the early societies, such as Burgess, Bruntsfield, Musselburgh and Blackheath, had foundation dates earlier than their first minutes, also a considerable part of the early minutes of the HCEG are missing.

When the Blackheath Club opened to non-masons, the Knuckle Club gradually faded away through lack of interest and the Club reverted to a normal Golf Club.

There is evidence of the masonic nature of the club from another source in the founding of golf clubs overseas by charter or diploma. *See* Chapter Ten. Most probably as a direct result of the deportment of regiments to overseas garrisons.

Scaife believes this was due to the admission of non-masons to the societies, owing to the decline in the number of golfers who were freemasons. It is surmised this led to the destruction of the early minutes to protect their masonic secrets.

He further elaborates on the historical fact that Thomas Longlands, a member of the Knuckle Club, suggested that they should have a gold medal designed, which would be played for in stroke play format.

This, being the oldest known golfing medal, became the forerunner of all future stroke play competitions that are now called *medal rounds*.

Scaife summarises the importance of these early golf societies that attracted wealthy and well-connected individuals in the following paragraph.

All devotees of the game of golf salute these early groups of masons who established and maintained organised golf for the first 100 years of its existence. If the game had not been formalised by freemasons, and associated inextricably with dining and general conviviality, it would probably only have survived as a quaint Scottish pastime, if at all, and certainly would never have developed into the game it is today. The debt owed by the golfer to freemasons of the 18th century is vast.

David Stirk in his book, 'Golf—History & Tradition' adds, *When men of money and power started to play golf, they could afford labour to improve golf links and caddies to carry their clubs. Groups of golfers played together on nearby land.*

These groups formed themselves into societies but before golfers formed societies, they had been in the habit of dining together after golf and this usually took place in a local tavern. It was here whilst dining that they considered the next day's play and set what wagers should be made.

The earliest golfing groups in Scotland and England were all designated societies, with the exception of The Company of Edinburgh Golfers. It was only later that most of these early societies became clubs.

A society and a club in these early years were very similar but a club is noted as meeting at a tavern with the members jointly paying the expenses and all being interested in the same pursuit. A society tended to meet under certain regulations and admission was usually guarded by ballot.

The significant feature of a society was not whom it admitted, but whom it kept out. Although the societies were careful about whom they allowed to become members, on the golf links they would play match-play with anyone who was a golfer.

Stirk continues, *The Royal Blackheath Golf Club—this was initially known as the Society of Golfers at Blackheath from a dedication of a portrait of William Innes, who was one of the Captains of Blackheath. In 1787 a local newspaper report on one of the Blackheath Medal days stated that the players were upwards of thirty gentlemen of the London Scots Society.*

It is recorded that, *All minutes prior to 1800 were lost in a fire at the end of the 19th century, although there is little evidence of a fire having occurred and all the valuable trophies that existed before 1800 have survived!*

Whilst the Society decided to change with the times they still behaved, according to Stirk, in a masonic manner, i.e., they issued diplomas and charters to golf clubs overseas, similar to Blackheath, thus giving them official status; a device used by Grand Lodge.

Masonic Lodges had a good communications network and the first rules of golf, formulated at Leith, were quickly circulated to all other masonic golf clubs, i.e. Blackheath, Perth, etc. Stirk maintained that one way in which the masons tried to keep control of events and decisions was to ensure that at least the Captain was always a freemason.

This they achieved by having the Captain elected by past captains, not by the committee; a method of selection that is still being practised by some clubs today.

In relation to the growth of other clubs in society, this is well covered by E Beresford Chancellor, in his book entitled 'The XVIII Century in London', which gives a brief history of the London clubs as follows:

In the 18th century, the social life of London began to take on an individual character linked with the industrial activity of that time. During the previous century the power of the monarch, then that of the great nobles and subsequently that of the Crown again was predominant, but in the 18th century became independent of exoteric influence.

From the commencement of the reign of Queen Anne in 1702 to the day when George III died in 1820, government by the people gradually became an established fact. This change in the administration of the country reflected itself both in the classes and the masses, as well as all kinds of institutions and customs.

During this period the middle classes became more powerful and more able to embrace the life from which they had before been rigidly excluded.

The club is essentially a British institution, although the club, as it is known today, has little in common with that of the 18th century. It was during the reign of Queen Anne that the club first came into existence.

In those early days, such clubs were usually held in taverns and their primary object was eating and drinking. Some of these became specifically designed buildings for this purpose, each club having its own distinctive patronage, such as politics, the arts, the stage and press etc.

The placing of many bets frequently took place in these establshments that were the daytime parlours of nobility and men of high stature. Hence it was not infrequent for some to be blackballed from membership. In London, there were many such clubs, notably Whites, Brooks, Boodles, Cocoa-Tree, Ozinda's, Scribblers' and the Royal Society.'

London has always been associated with club life, often involving gambling, which was frequented by the aristocracy and the rich and famous. Most of the clubs were in the heart of London but there were a few within an easy carriage drive from the city.

One such club was the Royal Blackheath Golf Club, which has always been associated with London Club life and has already been well covered, *see above*, but there was another golf club that also had close associations with Freemasonry and the social strata of the period, the Chislehurst Golf Club.

In their booklet of the history of 'The Camden Place Lodge', John Attenborough and William Mitchell give us a further insight into Edwardian England. Chislehurst Golf Club was founded in 1894—their clubhouse being in the 18th century mansion called Camden Place. 22 members of the Chislehurst Golf Club founded the Camden Place Lodge in 1904.

Their booklet states that, *In the late 19th century, Edwardian England was class-conscious, colourful and confident with merchant princes invading the aristocratic and sport-loving economy of West Kent, i.e. Chislehurst. At that time Edwardian Society with its great houses and many servants enabled Chislehurst to prosper. Whilst the churches and new railways were the natural meeting places for old and new residents, Chislehurst GC was also included in that category.*

Camden Place Lodge was first constituted in the Imperial Dining Room of Camden Place; Lord Amherst conducted the consecration ceremony. The Lodge has met in the Imperial Dining Room ever since. Meetings were conducted in evening dress with Champagne served for dinner; this continued until 1939. According to one of the founders, the 22 founding members were solid Victorian golfers, men of strong principles and determination who had acquired considerable wealth generally by their own efforts.

The Lodge logo features a golfer flailant surmounted by an imperial eagle. The lodge preamble states the proportion of non-members of the golf club should not exceed 50% of full members.

In view of the preponderance of golfers in the membership, it is surprising that the beneficial activity has not featured more prominently in the life of the Lodge. (Whereas) at Royal Blackheath, it is maintained that the prime purpose of the original seven holes across the heath was to build up an appetite for, and assist recovery from, the mighty masonic feasts for which the club was famous.

This is further amplified by W M Mitchell in his centenary history of Chislehurst Golf Club entitled, '100 Years of Golf at Camden Place'.

In this, he states, *In 1904 Camden Place acquired its own lodge of freemasons—No. 3042—consecrated on 27 June by Lord Amherst, Provincial Grand Master of Kent. Most of the 22 founders were golfers, including the Club Captain, his immediate predecessor and successor.*

The lodge crest features a golfer swinging his hickory-shafted club with panache. Freemasonry was at this time expanding as rapidly as golf.

One of Freemasonry's strengths is the ban on political and religious discussion and another is its positive emphasis on fellowship and charity, consequently, the Craft was widely held to perform a beneficent function in a society under the stress of change.

The new King, Edward VII, was himself a freemason and his brother the Duke of Connaught was the Grand Master of England.

The Lodge permanently booked the first Thursday in the months of November, December, February and March for their meeting every year, which were and still are held in Camden Place, the golf clubhouse.

The Lodge meetings were followed by a formal dinner initially in tailcoats or dinner jackets with claret being served after the port. Formal dining was a major feature of Edwardian life and golf was an admirable means of working up an appetite.

David Hamilton in his book entitled, 'Golf: Scotland's Game', he summarised the position as follows:

Most Gentlemen Golfers were members of another club, the masonic lodge. Freemasonry had started in Scotland in the 1500s when the stonemasons Craft attracted outside social members who patronised and gentrified the town Craft and encouraged its initiation rites.

To this, they added conviviality and benevolent activities. By the 1700s many gentlemen were masons and many were also golfers: thus, we need not be surprised that many Gentlemen Golfers were freemasons.'

There is a suggestion made that 18th century golf clubs were a façade concealing secret masonic lodges and that the clubs' evening gatherings were thinly disguised lodge meetings. This surmises that golf was not the most important, nor the most serious part, of the day's outings.

David Hamilton further suggests that the gaps in the early historical records of golf clubs were the result of golfing freemasons destroying their early secret minutes and records.

This thesis is thinly supported by the evidence, for instead of a conspiracy of destruction of minute books; the evidence is of the loss, decay and muddle. Analysis of any activity in the 18th century is hampered by such a loss of records.

Indeed, the Honourable Company's records and those of the R&A, the most important of the century, are remarkably well preserved. These records show that, far from the dinner (festive board) being the high point of the day, and essential for masonic cohesion, the Gentlemen Golfers organisation was plagued by the converse, the dreary problem of lack of interest.

David Hamilton further contends that, although the members tended to play golf, many departed for Edinburgh without taking dinner at Leith. As for secret rituals, privacy could hardly be great in the back room of a popular pub at this time, and any rites involved in the admission of new members, such as complex oaths of allegiance, would be difficult to conceal.

In any case, the evidence is that such activity would not be concealed. The masonic lodges had a high profile and were often involved in public ceremonies when their members and procedures were on open display.

But, according to Bernard Jones, this was exactly where the early lodges met, in taverns and public houses. Furthermore, masonic lodges are held at regular intervals and consequently, there would be many times when they did not dine after playing.

This aspect is further elaborated by H R Sharp in his 'History of the Lodge of Good Report No. 136', in which he states, *In the late 18th century lodge meetings were usually held in the upstairs room of a tavern with bare boards on the floor on which the Tyler (a Lodge Officer) would have drawn in chalk the tracing board.*

The tracing board is part of the lodge furniture used in their masonic rituals.

A wooden trestle table on which were placed candles would have taken a prominent place because the members would have sat around it during the meeting. After the masonic work (ritual)—the festive board was served on the same table.

It was then customary for lodges to hold meetings around the table at which they also dined. After the Grand Lodges united in 1813, ritual and the layout of the lodge room were standardised and the festive board became separated from the work of the Lodge.

It is further argued by David Hamilton that, *At Leith, on 2nd July 1768, the foundation stone of the Edinburgh Golfers' new clubhouse was laid with masonic ceremony, but this does not prove the masonic link.*

He continues, *When the Royal Infirmary of Edinburgh was opened in 1741, there was also a masonic procession and ceremony, and a little later the foundation stone of Aberdeen Royal Infirmary was ceremonially placed by the local 'Society of Free and Accepted Masons'.*

Masonic activity was simply part of public life in the 1700s: obsessive secrecy and concealed activity were to come later when, in Europe at least, the freemasons furtively opposed the traditional power of the aristocracy, hoping to elevate their own interests.

By the time this happened the early Scottish golf clubs were badly attended and in decay and incapable of any influence, secret or otherwise.

Hamilton, therefore, contends that it is unlikely our early club golfers had a hidden agenda of masonic activity.

All this may be true, but the ethics of Freemasonry has permeated into the laws of the game and this could not have happened without a close association of the two activities. Golf is one of the very few sports that was and still is self-regulating and this requires the complete honesty of the player at all times.

There is no doubt that in the early years, it was only the wealthy who could afford the cost of a golf ball, a feathery, and it was not until the production of the gutta-percha ball in 1848, which was considerably cheaper, that the game became attractive to the middle classes.

The artisans had always had a connection with golf through their caddying services and they continued to play outside the normal hours using old balls discarded by their employers.

Neil Laird has thrown further light on this subject in the website entitled 'Scottish Golf History'—The Role of Early Speculative Freemasons.

Several authorities cite the 'secrecy' of the freemasons for the absence of early Scottish golf history records, particularly of the Royal Burgess, but the evidence of these claims is weak. The main reason that members of early golf clubs were freemasons was because virtually all middle-class men of ability in Scotland in the century after 1717 were freemasons from senior law officers to skilled artisans as well as poets and writers, i.e.

Robert Burns and Sir Walter Scott were masons. From 1717 the Scottish stonemason freemasons, called operative masons, began to allow merchants and professional people, termed speculative masons, to join lodges or create their own. This practice spread elsewhere in the world, e.g. in France, Voltaire became a mason as did George Washington, who was buried with full masonic honours in America.

Scottish freemasons have kept the details of their activities from at least 1599 and now publish these on the web. It would be strange if they had destroyed their golf minutes to preserve the confidentiality of the members whilst keeping the lists of their Grand Masters and Council.

Extracts from the early minutes of five of the early (Golf) clubs are documented in the book 'Golf: A Royal and Ancient Game' *by Robert Clark and they read like the minutes of any modern club, parish council or tenant's association.*

They note banal details of admissions, competitions, match winners and other domestic arrangements; they do not indicate the heavy hand of masonic traditions. At best, they simply show that many important people who were involved with golf were freemasons and acknowledged as such.

The laying of the foundations of the first ever purpose-built golf clubhouse for the HCEG (Honourable Company of Edinburgh Golfers) *in 1768 on Leith Links is a case in point.* William St Clair of Roslyn conducted the ceremony.

The St Clairs of Roslyn were for many years the appointed hereditary masonic patrons in Scotland. However, it was not until William St Clair was elected the first Grand Master of the Grand Lodge of Scotland in 1736 that he achieved the title of Grand Master Mason.

At the time he was the Captain of Leith and a member of the St Andrews GC. He died in 1778 and is buried in the family's private Roslyn Chapel.

Neil Laird continues that *The First Minute Books of The HCEG and The R & A of St Andrews, which contained the most prominent masons of the time, are still extant. The minutes of the Royal Blackheath GC, which was also strongly masonic, were destroyed in a fire.*

The Royal Burgess GS has its minutes back to 1773, and it is not certain whether there were any minutes kept before then. The only early minute books that definitely existed, but whose fate is unknown, are the five books (prior to 1874) of the Bruntsfield Links GS and those of Royal Musselburgh GC (also before 1874), neither of which clubs displayed any particular masonic connections. However, the minutes of these clubs were then lost en masse.

The freemasons' tradition, (which) is of self-improvement ('making a good man better') and of self-determination for artisans and professionals was adopted by our modern educational institutions, trade associations and professional bodies.

Equally important is the major role that the freemasons played in making golf the game we know today. From 1717 onward, when speculative masons began to be recruited to Scottish lodges, many early Scottish links golfers were masons, who played their part in creating the golf club and organising golf into what it has become today.

The Grand Lodge of Scotland, which was founded in 1736, is the third Grand Lodge of Freemasonry after the English (1717) and the Irish (1725). Interestingly, 1736 is one year after the published foundation date for the Burgess Club in Edinburgh. It is therefore possible that the Burgess masons did not join the Grand Lodge of Scotland.

There is little doubting the masonic origins of the Club, as many people point out, their main and present-day tradition of shaking in, whereby the Captain of the Burgess can admit anyone on a shake of his hand, admits little other interpretation.

It is therefore likely that as the foundation of the Burgess Club was in 1735, i.e. before the foundation of the Grand Lodge of Scotland, the masons of the Burgess Club did not join the Grand Lodge but continued to observe masonic traditions.

The freemasons use of the black ball to exclude undesirable members appears more enlightened when viewed against the elections for members of parliament (that) was by a show of hands or by appointment or by a small number of constituency freemen and often subject to monetary influence.

The freemasons do not deserve the charge, sometimes levelled at them, of securing their own self-interests unduly and plotting secret world domination. Freemasonry is due its credit for past contributions to our social, political, economic and sporting life.

If there had been any conspiracy here it would appear to be on the part of those making fanciful claims for the destruction of golfing records and other shenanigans, without a single witness for the prosecution.

There was initial division in Freemasonry and, as noted above, the first Grand Lodge in the world, the Premier Grand Lodge of England, was established in 1717. 34 years later a group of Irish masons founded a competitor, the Atholl Grand Lodge.

The newcomer claimed that its rival had made innovations in historic masonry. Consequently, they styled themselves *Antients* and dismissed the Premier Grand Lodge as *Moderns*. It was not until 1813 that the three Grand Lodges became united as the United Grand Lodge of England.

The above demonstrates the close association of the golf club with Freemasonry mainly through the social strata that pervaded golf during this period. However, it is not clear which came first, the golf club or Freemasonry; they were certainly developing in parallel and at a similar rate.

Chapter Seven
The Growth of Freemasonry

The history of Freemasonry has many facets but in relation to this quest to discover its association with the foundation of golf clubs, it is best commenced with extracts from, 'The Genesis of Freemasonry' by David Harrison.

The search for lost treasure by the Knights Templar, within the ruins of Solomon's Temple symbolises the search for lost knowledge, a theme that resounds within the ritual and factual history of Freemasonry.

King Solomon's Temple can be seen as symbolising strength and divine secret knowledge, whilst the masonic lodge, which is constructed in the image of the Temple, is the place where masons come to receive instruction on mathematics, geometry and astrology.

This ultimate wisdom reserved for masons has thus been linked to the ancient medieval Templar order going back as far as Solomon, David and Egypt.

The Knights Templar was a semi-religious order whose brotherhood became very powerful and respected. They were so trusted by kings and nobility that they became the bankers of the European countries in which they operated.

Eventually, this caused much concern to the King of France who believed that they had become more powerful than he, which was not acceptable. Consequently, King Philippe IV ordered the arrest of all Templar members on Friday 13 October 1307. This became known as *Black Friday* and has been a source of superstition ever since.

Subsequently, the Pope dissolved the Order in 1312 and in 1314 Jacques de Molay, the Grand Master of the Templars, was burned at the stake. It is believed that remnants of the Templar Order escaped to Scotland by boat landing in the Western Isles and that the surviving members found support from Robert Bruce, the Scottish King, who defeated the English at Bannockburn in 1314.

It is speculated that this Templar Order may have influenced the formation of Freemasonry in Scotland,

Robert Cooper has proved this speculation substantially incorrect in his book, 'The Rosslyn Hoax'. The Templars left no trace of their arrival in Argyll nor of their integration within Scotland.

Neither did they take any part in the Battle of Bannockburn as he advises they would have been too old to fight. Furthermore, the Knights Templar died out before Freemasonry in Scotland became formalised.

David Harrison further explains that *Scotland had far more documentary evidence of early Freemasonry than England, which has possibly influenced their speculation.*

England did not have permanent lodges like the ones in Scotland until the late 17th century, whereas the Lodge of

Edinburgh and Kilwinning can be traced back to the 16th century; it has minute books dating back to 1599.

The evidence is that they originated as purely operative lodges but became infiltrated by speculative masons during the civil war (mid–17th century).

Harrison continues, *Early English lodges were considered temporary meetings that came together for special gatherings and then disappeared as quickly as they were formed.*

Elias Ashmole, who was a native of Staffordshire, had been present at Worcester during the early part of 1646 where he had been offered the post of Captain in Lord Ashley's Regiment of Foot in the Royalist Infantry. He moved to Cheshire, after its surrender to parliamentary forces in July, where Peter Mainwaring, his father-in-law, lived.

It may have been here that Ashmole learnt of the Lodge in Warrington and felt it important enough to be initiated along with Henry Mainwaring. Colonel Henry Mainwaring was a close relative of Ashmole's father-in-law and his entry into the Craft may have been politically motivated, as Ashmole was a Royalist and Mainwaring a supporter of parliament.

Scotland's earliest recorded speculative freemason on English soil was Sir Robert Moray, who was made a freemason in Newcastle-upon-Tyne in 1641, by members of the Lodge of Edinburgh who, like Moray, were in the Scottish army.

Moray and Ashmole were founding members of The Royal Society, which was formed in 1660, and both would have found their links to Freemasonry very beneficial at this time of political uncertainty.

Even at this early stage of Freemasonry, there was a connection to the military for as Harrison declares, *Colonel Francis Columbine who was the Commander of the 10th Foot Guards, was the Provincial Grand Master of Cheshire.*

His lodge also contained a number of other local, prominent military men, i.e. Captain Hugh Warburton and Colonel Herbert Laurence, who served as Wardens, and Captain John Vanberg and Captain Robert Frazier.

Harrison continues *that the association of the Knights Templar with Scottish Freemasonry appears on the Knights Templar and masonic tombstones in the ruins of the Chapel of Holyrood House at Edinburgh and infers that from the interpretation of the iconography displayed masonry has been a pure, though mysterious, descent from the ancient mysteries.*

There is a similar common occurrence of stylised skulls and crossbones on Scottish gravestones in the churchyards of Kilmartin, Leith and the Chapel Yard Cemetery in Inverness, some having links to known freemasons. The churchyard in Kilmartin also has a number of gravestones from the medieval period, thought to be of Templar influence.

The Rosslyn Chapel, which was built by St Clair as a private family chapel, also displays carvings related to the Knights Templars. Some historians dispute their relevance to the Knights Templars but there can be no doubt that they exist and are carved alongside many other masonic symbols.

The Rosslyn Chapel is an important link in the history of Scottish Freemasonry and its mysteries still leave many unanswered questions.

The dispute between the Whigs and the Jacobites was not a deterrent to becoming a freemason and Harrison gives us some background to this when he states: *There were both Whigs and Jacobites included in English Freemasonry, a political inclusiveness that was evident in Scotland and Wales.*

A powerful Jacobite freemason was James Radcliffe, Earl of Derwentwater, who was beheaded in 1716 for his involvement in the Jacobite Rebellion of 1715.

His brother Charles, who was also a freemason and a friend of the Duke of Wharton's associate, the Earl of Lichfield, had escaped to France, where he passed into legend as an early French Grand Master.

Charles Radcliffe returned to Britain during the second Jacobite uprising of 1745, only to be executed the following year after the failure of the rebellion. The Earl of Winton was also a prominent freemason who took part in the Rebellion of 1715 but after his trial, he escaped to Europe where he died (in 1749).

In 1745 many prominent Scottish freemasons rallied to the Jacobite cause, i.e. William Boyd, 4th Earl of Kilmarnock, who had been Grand Master of the Scottish Grand Lodge in 1742 and was executed in 1746. His son Lord Boyd fought for the Hanoverians and became the Grand Master in 1751.

Lord Elcho, son of James (Wemyss, the 4th) Earl of Wemyss, who was Grand Master in 1743, also joined the Jacobite Rebellion of 1745 and tried to switch his allegiance after the failure of the Rebellion, was excluded from his titles and estates and exiled.

Another was (George Mackenzie, the 3rd) Earl of Cromartie, who had been Grand Master in 1737, was captured at Culloden but escaped execution due to his wife's successful plea to George II. Other prominent Scottish freemasons were anti-Jacobite, i.e., George Drummond, the Lord Provost of Edinburgh, who was Grand Master in 1752.

According to some historians, Bonnie Prince Charlie was the Grand Master of Scottish Freemasonry. The Antients were Jacobites and the moderns were Hanoverian. However, Harrison records there is no firm evidence to support these claims.

Harrison then clarifies the development of the Craft and continues, *that William Preston was born in Edinburgh 1742 first working as a printer before moving to London in 1762 where he entered journalism, becoming Editor of the 'London Chronicle'. He joined a lodge under the jurisdiction of the Antients.*

The lodge had been formed by a number of Scottish freemasons from Edinburgh, who had planned to create a London lodge under the jurisdiction of the Grand Lodge of Scotland, but this was rejected on the grounds that it might interfere with the Premier (Modern) Grand Lodge of England.

So, the Scottish Grand Lodge recommended Scottish masons to the Antient Grand Lodge instead, who welcomed them.'

William Preston was a masonic scholar and is known for his masonic lectures. He was responsible for drawing the perception of Freemasonry away from the bar and dining table and giving it a more cerebral appeal. He was also associated with the movement of masonic meetings from taverns into dedicated masonic buildings, known as masonic temples.

Harrison then gives a potted history of the development of Freemasonry in the United Kingdom.

In 1732, the Grand Lodge of Ireland demanded that all lodges under its jurisdiction should apply for a warrant and in 1740 the demand was issued again. In 1805, another feud within Irish Freemasonry erupted, when the Grand Lodge of Ulster appeared. This rebellion was short-lived when it conformed in 1814.

In Scotland, Freemasonry was celebrated for its ancient links with a tradition that King James I was a freemason. In 1721, Desaguliers visited a lodge at St Mary's Chapel in Edinburgh, which may have inspired him to revise the ritual, adopting certain themes and symbolism, i.e. the adoption of the skull and crossbones, which became embedded in the additional 3rd degree raising ritual, possibly derived from Scottish grave iconography.

In 1723, a copy of Anderson's Constitutions was presented to the Lodge of Dunblane. These actions were perhaps friendly approaches to establish contact, but it's clear the politics of Freemasonry was being played, especially so soon after the foundation of the Premier (Modern) Grand Lodge of England, in London (1717).

The Scottish Grand Lodge was officially formed on 15 October 1736 at St Mary's Chapel. The first Grand Master was William St Clair of Roslyn, but a number of Scottish lodges claimed independence, i.e. Melrose, Haughfoot, Glasgow, St John, Dundee, Scone and Perth.

The Scottish Grand Lodge opened communication with the Premier (Modern) Grand Lodge in 1740, but along with the Irish Grand Lodge, was officially to recognise the Antient Grand Lodge instead when it was formed in 1751.

The Earl of Blessington, who had been Grand Master of the Irish Grand Lodge in 1738, became Grand Master of the Antients (in 1756). This symbolised the close association between the Antients and the Irish Grand Lodge. Other aristocratic Grand Masters followed, i.e. (John Murray the 3rd) Duke of Atholl, who was installed in 1771 as the Grand Master.

(John Murray,) the 4th Duke of Atholl was installed Grand Master in 1775 after the 3rd Duke's death, and again in 1792 after the death of the Earl of Antrim. In 1813, he stood down in favour of Prince Edward, the Duke of Kent, whose involvement paved the way for the unification of the Antients and the Moderns.

John Hamill, in his article 'Working as One' expands on the differing Grand Lodges that were in existence at this time and their progress towards the formation of the United Grand Lodge of England.

The Antients Grand Lodge was formed in 1751, most likely instigated by Irish brethren who had been unable to gain entry to lodges under the Premier Grand Lodge that was formed in 1717. This marked a period when two Grand Lodges existed side by side, an uncomfortable situation for both lodges with much rivalry. This rivalry did not last too long for many London freemasons had a foot in both camps.

In 1801, there was a serious attempt to unify the two but there were some members who did not wish this to happen resulting in one prominent member of the Antients, Francis Columbine Daniel, being expelled for being in both Grand Lodges.

Daniel believed this to have been engineered by Thomas Harper who was the (Deputy) Grand Master of the Antients at the time. Harper himself had been active in both Grand Lodges in 1796 being a Grand Steward in the Premier Grand Lodge whilst being the Deputy Grand Secretary of the Antients.

Daniel forced the Premier Grand Lodge to recognise the fact and Harper was expelled in 1803, which brought all discussions about a Union to a halt.

In 1806, the Prince of Wales (later King George IV), who had been Grand Master of the Premier Grand Lodge since 1791, was elected Grand Master Mason of the Grand Lodge of Scotland, appointing the Earl of Moira as his acting Grand Master, as he was in England.

This led to the setting up of a joint committee in 1809 to explore the possibility of forming a Union of the two Grand Lodges. Harper was still the Deputy Grand Master of the Antients and held a strong influence in the absence of the Grand Master, the 4th Duke of Atholl.

To overcome his objections, Harper was welcomed back into the Premier Grand Lodge in 1810 and negotiations for a Union continued. These continued for another four years, largely delayed by the Antients' grand secretary, Robert Leslie, who was firmly against the Union.

The situation was resolved when both Grand Masters resigned in 1813, the Prince of Wales being succeeded by his brother the Duke of Sussex and the Duke of Atholl being succeeded by another Royal brother the Duke of Kent.

Within six weeks, the two brothers had resolved all difficulties and drawn up Articles of Union. The great ceremony of the Union took place at Freemasons Hall on 27 December 1813 and the Duke of Sussex was installed as Grand Master of the United Grand Lodge of England.

Whilst the growth of Freemasonry would appear to have little to do with its influence on the foundation of golf clubs, golf was expanding in a similar time frame in Scotland but at a slower rate in England. This was thought to be due to the due to lack of good communication. Many of the principal players were committed to both.

It had always been assumed that it was the establishment of the railways that was responsible for the rapid growth of golf clubs in England, but Michael Morrison in his recent book entitled 'The Great English Golf Boom' advises otherwise.

He rightly points out in his book that the expansion of the railways preceded the expansion of golf by at least 40 years and it was the invention of the bicycle plus the introduction of the Haskell ball that enabled beginners to better enjoy the game which drove the growth of golf in England.

All three culminated at the same time and caused a great demand for new courses and the development of the game.

When the two Grand Lodges of England unified Freemasonry became more organised and politically stable. Likewise, the game of golf, its club structures and its administration became more organised and consolidated under the auspices of its premier club, the Royal & Ancient Golf Club of St Andrews.

Whilst Freemasonry lodges continued to expand throughout the 19th century, golf suffered a serious decline in the first half due to economic pressure caused by the aftermath of the French Revolution and the fear of invasion.

This changed dramatically in the second half with the Industrial Revolution, easier travel following the growth of railway networks and the cost of golf balls coming within the remit of the new middle classes.

The game was seen by this new middle class not only as a worthy sporting exercise but also as a social means of mixing with wealthy industrialists, financiers and property entrepreneurs who would fashion the future of the United Kingdom.

The extent of the growth can be measured by the fact that in 1799 there were only 12 golf clubs in the UK. By 1851 this had increased to 24, but by 1899, this had risen to 1,276.

The military played little part in the growth of golf clubs during the second half of the 19th century, but prior to that, the game had been dominated by the wealthier members of society, many of whom were regimental officers or had a military background. Their pivotal role came when Freemasonry and the game of golf were expanded overseas.

Chapter Eight
The Influence of the Military During the 18th and 19th Centuries

Whilst it has been established that early military field lodges had little or no direct link to the foundation of golf clubs, they undoubtedly laid the foundation for the formation of subsequent military lodges that continue to this day.

In this chapter, their link to golf and Freemasonry is explored further, in particular to their posting of garrisons on links and commons where golf was being played.

Some clubs and early golfing societies had a direct link with the militia and that of the Dunbar Golfing Society is well recorded by J V Harris in his publication, 'Dunbar Golf'.

In this, he stated that, *Although the masonic influence over golf was questioned, the connection between Freemasonry and organised golf existed and in the Dunbar case the connection was a strong and proven one.*

Dunbar was a garrison town with many troops barracked there over the years. The West Barns Links were commandeered by the military during and after the

Napoleonic Wars and the Society moved to Dunbar Links, but there is no record of golf (being played) on the Dunbar Links before 1850.

As the Society was setting down its regulations, the long and proud military tradition of Dunbar was underway. There had been stables in Dunbar for Dragoons even before 1794, the Dunbar Volunteer Militia being formed in 1762.

When a battery was built on Lammer Island in 1781–82, the volunteer soldiers were under the command of Major George Hay of Belton, one of the 26 founder members of the Dunbar Golfing Society.

These soldiers became the 'Dunbar Defensive Company', numbering 73 men initially and Christopher Middlemass, the prominent member of the Dunbar Golfing Society, later assumed control from Hay.

1782 the 'South Fencibles' and its artillery camped on West Barns Links followed by the 'Essex Light Dragoons' and a regiment of Black Horse. With the outbreak of the Napoleonic Wars (1792–1815) the East Lothian Yeomanry cavalry was stationed at Dunbar with the 4th Dunbar Troop comprising 75 men, raised in 1797 by Robert Hay of Sprott.

This is the Regiment most associated with the town, it later became the Lothian & Border Horse, then Lothian & Berwickshire Yeomanry Cavalry in 1888, and finally incorporated into the Royal Tank Corps.

J V Harris continues, *1794 saw the encampment on West Barns Links of two battalions of foot soldiers and a regiment of Dragoons. Two years later, there was a cavalry camp comprising regiments of the Cambridge Fencibles, the Windsor Foresters and the East Lothian Yeomanry.*

This culminated in 1803 with the greatest military force ever assembled on these shores being encamped on West Barns Links under General Sir George Don. This almost continuous military occupation of West Barns Links extended after 1815 and ensured no record of golf there until almost a century after the formation of the Dunbar Golfing Society.

The West Barns residents created the demand for the game, (and) with a population swollen by the demands from a major powerhouse of local industry, Dunbar Golf Club was formed in 1856. Despite many attempts, no umbilical link has been found between the two organisations.

Another club with military connections is Lanark and the following has been extracted from their website.

From its beginning, the Club has had connections with the army. In the early days, the militia was encamped on what is today's practice ground and when Winston Barracks was built nearby, a close affinity between the Club and the Cameronian Regiment was established.

It is recorded that, *Several of the Club's trophies have been presented by the HLI (Highland Light Infantry) and Cameronians, including the 1893 mess silverware, which is played for as the Army Cup each year in the invitational foursomes competition.*

The original founders of the Club in 1851 were Robert Lithgow, William Lithgow, John Vassie and Thomas Purdie. Sir W C Anstruther was another prominent member.

The course is laid out on 'The Moor and the Militia' camped almost yearly on the course with the men's quarters on the 13th and 14th fairways and the officer's quarters on the Knoll beside the trees on the 15th. The town council, who regarded the militia with a mercenary affection, owned the Moor.

The militia paid a handsome rent and brought trade to the town. The militia eventually moved away, thanks to Lord Haldane's reorganisation of the army and after the Club had received a 25-year lease on the course.

Col. William (Bill) Gibson in his article on 'The First Golf Club in Ireland' published in *Through the Green*, he mentions that *he had been researching a major work that arose from a clue given to him in 1989 by Dr Steven Reid who sent him evidence of the creation of a masonic lodge in 1762.*

The Grand Lodge of Ireland had issued a warrant to lodge No. 11 in the 1st Battalion Royal Scots Regiment on [h] November 1732. Lodge No. 11 was listed as one of 37 lodges warranted in Ireland, meeting at Bray, Co. Wicklow. When the Lodge was first formed in 1732 most were non-commissioned ranks.

A further Masonic (Travelling) Warrant No. 381 was granted to the Regiment on 7 September 1762, which resulted in another 23 members being admitted on this date, none of which were commissioned officers.

Bray Golf Club was formed on 23 October 1762 and their military barracks were close by. The commanding officer in 1762 was Col. Robert Dalrymple Horn Elphinstone, the Captain of the Company of Gentlemen Golfers, later to become the Honourable Company of Edinburgh Golfers, and his presence would have had a significant influence on the formation of the golf club at Bray.

Whilst Gibson claims Bray to be the first golf club in Ireland, it should be noted that Harry Carr previously recorded Trinity College GC in Dublin as being formed in 1724.

Col. Gibson continues, *the Royal Scots Regiment that was stationed in Bray from 1744 to 1762 reveals the names of several officers who were members of the Company of Gentlemen Golfers (HCEG), these being: Captain Robert Mirrie; Lieutenant James Masterton; Captain James Cunningham; Ensign Charles Congleton/Congalton; Ensign Hon. James Stuart and Ensign James Lumsdaine/Lumisden. Cunningham and Stuart served in Ireland between December 1748 and May 1757.*

Masterton and Congleton were in Bray between 1762 and 1765. The general officer commanding forces in Ireland in 1762 was Lieutenant-General John Leslie, 10th Earl of Rothes, admitted a member of the Company of Gentlemen Golfers in 1749.

The Colonel of the Royal Scots Regiment in 1762 was Lieutenant-General James St Clair, a founder member of the Society of St Andrews Golfers (R&A) in 1754. James St Clair was at that time the proprietor of Dysart Castle in Fife, a property belonging to William St Clair, one of the legendary figures in the early history of golf and of Freemasonry.

When the entry conditions for the Company of Gentlemen Golfers' silver club competition were amended to exclude the right for the winner to become the captain of the club in the ensuing year, Col. Robert Dalrymple Horn Elphinstone was Captain of the Company.

In doing so he had in mind the sizeable number of non-commissioned officers of the Royal Scots Regiment who were active freemasons and acquainted with the game of golf from their service at Bray, many of whom would have been discharged from the army at the end of the Seven Years War in 1763.

Other golfing regiments that served in Ireland prior to 1762 were:

42nd Regiment	1748–1756
39th Regiment	1749–1754; 1758–1769
25th Regiment	1749–1755
27th Regiment	1749–1756
18th Regiment	1749–1755; 1757–1767
26th Regiment	1749–1755; 1757–1767
55th Regiment	1756–1757
59th Regiment	1756–1765
52nd Regiment	1757–1765
58th Regiment	1757–1758; 1763–1771
83rd Regiment	1758–1762
120th Regiment	1762–1763
122nd Regiment	1762–1763

Col. Gibson continues, *that the Royal Scots were posted to Ireland in 1727 and remained there until 1743 when it moved to Flanders at the outset of war in support of the succession of Maria Theresa to the throne of Austria. They returned to Ireland in 1749 and remained until 1768 when the regiment embarked for Gibraltar.*

It is clear there is a strong connection with the formation of the golf club by the Royal Scots Guards and, as the first members of the Bray GC may have been largely made up of non-commissioned officers, it must be assumed that many of them were also members of Lodge No. 11.

Furthermore, William H Gibson records in another article published in *Through the Green*, that Archibald Montgomerie, the 13th Earl of Eglinton, who was the Lord Lieutenant of Ireland at the time, was a frequent member of Bray Golf Club and played with Major Robert Harrington and Lieutenant Andrew Smith of the 2nd Battalion Royal Lanarkshire Militia.

The Earl is also recorded as playing an exhibition match against Sir James Baird, with the Prince of Wales, later King Edward VII, being an interested observer. Subsequently, the Prince, who was at that time an officer in the Grenadier Guards, also played a match against Sir James Baird. The Prince later became Captain of the R&A in 1863.

Another golf club in Ireland to have a military background is the Curragh Golf Club, which was founded in Kildare as the result of a military encampment nearby. Many regiments were posted at this encampment and comprised: the 2nd Battalion 60th Regiment; Cork North Militia; Dublin Co. Militia; 2/10th Regiment; 2/14th Regiment; 2/16th Regiment; 2/18th Regiment; 76th Regiment; North Lincolnshire Militia and 2nd Staffordshire Regiment'.

The (Royal) Curragh Golf Club dates from 1858 but the 13th Earl of Eglinton was reported playing on the Curragh six years earlier. Consequently, the Club claims to be the oldest course in Ireland, but this is disputed according to previous claims made by Bray GC and Trinity GC, Dublin.

The camp was evacuated by the British Army in 1922 and handed over to the Irish Defence Forces. Since then, the Club has maintained a tradition of military and civilian involvement in its management. Every second year, a member of the armed forces is made Captain of the Club.

The Royal prefix was granted to the Club in 1910 but when the Irish Free State came into being the title was repudiated. The members voted for its royal status to be revived in 2013.

Some of the regiments when garrisoned abroad took their golf and Freemasonry with them. This is ably covered by Michael Baigent and Richard Leigh in their book 'The Temple and the Lodge' who records that in 1692, one of the regiments, the Scots Brigade, was stationed in Dunkerque.

It is further recorded that the unit included many officers who had an interest in Freemasonry, particularly John Claverhouse, who was Viscount Dundee and a Grand Master of a Templar group or similar in Scotland.

When he died on the battlefield he was found wearing Templar Regalia, this being the Grand Cross of the order. This suggests that Templar had survived in Scotland, which poses the question as to why the Earl of Mar, who supported the English parliament, succeeded John Claverhouse as Grand Master on his death. for he was not recognised as a Jacobite until 1715.

The Templar cult was now only being kept alive in France but when Bonnie Prince Charlie decided to return to Scotland to regain what he considered to be his rightful heir, he did not have the promised support of France. This left him in a very weak position.

He nevertheless advanced south to Derby, hoping that he would gain volunteers to support his quest, but this was not to be. He therefore had to retreat and, with the Hanoverian troops in pursuit, his situation deteriorated, resulting in their annihilation at the Battle of Culloden on 16 April 1746 by Prince William's army under the direction of the Duke of Cumberland.

Charles Edward Stewart (Bonnie Prince Charlie) fled into exile and never returned. The Jacobite's dream of restoring the Stuarts to the British throne was ended. Some of the captured Jacobites were deported or banished and others were executed, including Charles Radclyffe.

Jacobite Freemasonry effectively died out after the Battle of Culloden and any political allegiance to the Stuart bloodline was ended.

The first five lodges in the British Army were formed in the 1730s and these increased to 29 by 1755. Many of the regiments had field lodges but these were not chartered by the Grand Lodge of England but by the Irish Grand Lodge whose ceremonies in part were characteristic of Jacobite Freemasonry.

The Duke of Cumberland who won the Battle of Culloden was the younger son of George II and a freemason, likewise General Sir John Ligonier, the most senior officer in the British Army. One of his officers was Lord Jeffrey Amherst who subsequently became the most important British officer of the age.

Whilst commanding many regiments he also established their field lodges. Amherst's sponsor was Lionel Sackville, the 1st Duke of Dorset, who had two sons, Charles and George, both of whom were also active freemasons and set up their own field lodges in their own regiments.

George became the Master of his own field lodge and one of his Wardens was Lieutenant-Colonel Edward Cornwallis, who was made the Governor of Nova Scotia in 1750; where he founded their first lodge. He was also a Grand Master of the Irish Grand Lodge.

A further example of the military's masonic influence on golf clubs is given by John Downs in his book 'The London Scottish Golf Club'.

A meeting took place on 4 July 1859 in The Freemason's Tavern in London for the formation of the 'London Scottish Rifle Volunteers'. The tavern was not large but large enough to take the handful of Scots gathered there, comprising members and friends of the Caledonian and Highland Societies who were based in London.

Lord Elcho, who was to become the Earl of Wemyss and March, was in the chair and called the meeting to order. There was one significant resolution to be debated and it was read aloud:

That as the present condition of affairs on the continent of Europe may lead to complications that will render it impossible for Great Britain, with due regard to her material interests and high station among nations, to maintain a position of neutrality, it is expedient that Scottish residents in London and its neighbourhood be invited to participate in strengthening the defensive resources of the country by forming a volunteer rifle corps, to be designated the 'London Scottish Rifle Volunteers'. It was carried unanimously, and Lord Elcho was appointed the commanding officer.

When HM Queen Victoria inspected the Regiment at a review in Hyde Park, in June 1860, the 'London Scottish' had 500 members and 100 supporters in the form of voluntary members. The men were ready and fighting fit but the complications in Europe did not emerge and they were not called upon until the First World War.

In the intervening period, their attention was diverted to golf and John Downs continues, *on 5 November 1864, after the Rifle Match arranged by the National Rifle Association, a meeting was held on Wimbledon Common to arrange for a golf club to be formed. There were 16 founder members, most of whom were 'London Scottish Rifle Volunteers'. The founder members were:*

Lt Col Lord Elcho MP—President
Pte A G Mackenzie—Captain
Pte R E Dudgeon MD—Vice-Captain
Armourer Sgt James Kerr—Treasurer
Pte R H Usher
Pte J C Fowlie
Pte A Cheyne
Captain S Flood Page
Sir James Hope Grant
Mr W Fordyce MP
Mr R G Suttie
Lt W Porteous
Lt R Fisher
Mr Darrock
Hon C Carnegie MP
Pte D C Sommerville'

Downs continues, *The Club was founded in 1864 by Lord Elcho and adopted by the 'London Scottish Rifle Volunteers' in 1866. It is believed that the Club was started to induce men to join the London Scottish Regiment.*

Initially, they retired to Mrs Doggett's Cottage for their victuals after play, but the room became too small and in 1871 the Club moved to an extension of the shooting house, the HQ of the 'London Scottish Rifle Volunteers'. This was on Wimbledon Common and known as the 'Iron House'. A new clubhouse was built in 1897.

The military origins of golf on the common are immediately apparent as one walks into the clubhouse. The lockers, preserved in the main, are rifle cabinets from the last century. Furthermore, the military association is confirmed by the appointment of one of the three Common Conservators always by the Secretary of State for Defence.

The Volunteer Corps subsequently comprised of Wimbledon's Own, London Scottish, the Civil Service and the First Surrey.

Golfers in those early years were predominantly exiled Scots, who had elected to come on a civilising mission southward, who had brought their national game with them, and who had chosen with magnanimous disinterestedness to bear the self-imposed burden of teaching their English brethren the game.

The history of Wimbledon Common Golf Club has photographs of their voting box and black ball that was used to select new members, the design of which is identical to that used in Freemasonry; likewise, the use of a gavel at their dinners.

Hugh Grieve, one of their members, listed the sequence of formation of the three different clubs as follows:

1865 –	The formation of the London Scottish Golf Club, although it is believed that records reveal that it was played on the common before 1865.
1880 –	The approximate date for the formation of Royal Wimbledon Golf Club; the Golfer's Handbook states 1865.
1908 –	The formation of Wimbledon Common Golf Club.

Hugh's understanding is that the gentry of Wimbledon who played golf, tired of Lord Elcho and volunteer soldiers, who did not pay any subscriptions to the London Scottish Club and decided to form their own Club. Lord Elcho ruled and his decision was resented.

Consequently, Wimbledon Common Golf Club became a breakaway from the London Scottish Golf Club by the towns' people, who wished to have their own golf club. Royal Wimbledon Golf Club has its own separate course, whilst Wimbledon Common Golf Club and London Scottish Golf Club share the same 18-hole course.

There may well be a masonic lodge attached to Royal Wimbledon but currently, it has little to do with the golf club.

Clapham Common Golf Club is another club with a military connection. it is believed to have been formed in 1873, although officially recorded as founded in May 1874. It was played over the Battersea end of Clapham Common and is thought likely that the 25 founder members agreed to form a club in late 1873.

Their founder President was Eugene H Cronin MD, who presented the Club's first trophy in 1875, a gold medal. The first Club Captain was James Kerr, who was a member of the London Scottish. Charles Cundell, Alexander Grace, John

Taylor, George Molesworth, Robert Morton and Alfred Siordet were also founder members.

The initial 9-hole course was played over the common and lengthened in 1881 by golf architect, Tom Dunn.

The common, which was open to the public, became too busy for it to continue to be used as a golf course safely, and could only continue to be played with many restrictions. During the First World War part of the course was turned over to allotments.

It was again requisitioned during the Second World War for the war effort, both for food production and military exercise, and sadly did not recover thereafter. However, the Club carried on and now play their golf over the Mitcham Common Golf Course.

From the above, there can be no doubt as to the influence that the military garrisons had on the formation of these golf clubs and in some cases the formation of Freemasonry lodges as well.

The close association of all three disciplines, i.e. golf, Freemasonry and the military, is noted but as to which influenced the other first is hard to determine. The fact that certain members of society were engaged in all three became the driving force.

Chapter Nine
The Spread of Freemasonry
Around the World

Freemasonry, which had been long associated with the ruling classes, was subliminally carried overseas by the early settlers and officers of regiments garrisoned in foreign lands. It served as a bond between the officers and their men in those strange lands and the early settlers before being permeated into the culture of the colonies.

Freemasonry was spread in the colonies by the early settlers such as John Skene who, as a member of an Aberdeen Lodge, emigrated and settled in New Jersey in 1682, where he later became its Deputy Governor. Another English emigrant to America, John Belcher, became a freemason on a visit to England in 1704.

On his return to the American colonies, he became a very successful merchant and eventually was made the Governor of Massachusetts and New Hampshire in 1730 to 1741. He too was one of the early promoters of Freemasonry in America and his son was particularly instrumental in its expansion.

The earliest recorded notice of Freemasonry in North America was in 'The Pennsylvania Gazette' on 8 December 1730. The newspaper was owned by Benjamin Franklin who became a Freemason in February 1731 and the Provincial Master of Pennsylvania in 1734. There were no records of any American lodges before 1720s.

The first recorded American lodge was founded in Philadelphia; however, St John's Lodge of Boston is the first officially chartered American lodge recorded by the Grand Lodge of England as founded in 1733.

Subsequently, Provincial Grand Lodges were warranted by the Grand Lodge of England in Massachusetts, New York, Pennsylvania and South Carolina. Local lodges were also founded in other states.

On 5 June 1730, the Premier Grand Lodge of England appointed Daniel Coxe, Provincial Grand Master for New York, New Jersey and Pennsylvania, thus giving the first official masonic recognition of the English colonies.

As no earlier records exist before 1730, this year is recognised as the commencement date of American Freemasonry.

By the 1730s, the Grand Lodge of England had begun to take a burgeoning interest in North America and to *warrant lodges* there; they were called affiliates. In 1732, General James Oglethorpe with 150 settlers founded a colony at the mouth of the Savannah River in Georgia and two years later became the master of Georgia's first Freemasonic lodge, Solomon's Lodge No. 1 in Savannah.

It is interesting that the oldest golf club in America is the Savannah Golf Club, which was founded in 1794. The likelihood of there being a masonic connection is quite strong.

In Chapter Eight, we referred to Lord Amherst's involvement in Freemasonry and this led to his officers being influenced by the Craft, many becoming members of the fraternity. This created a bond with fellow freemasons and secured a strong fighting force committed to serving one another and their colonial counterparts.

Many well-known Americans became freemasons including George Washington. Others, who were not practising freemasons were exposed to the influence of Freemasonry and officers of the British Army, who were freemasons, encouraged the fledgling lodges already established in the colonies. Thus, promoting the moral culture of Freemasonry around the globe.

Sadly, the records of these regimental field lodges were not kept, consequently, it is not possible to establish who were practising freemasons among the colonial officers of the British Army. It is recorded above that these early field lodges were mostly constituted under warrants issued by the Grand Lodge of Ireland.

The first Provincial Grand Lodge of America formed in 1778, under the jurisdiction of England's Grand Lodge, was named the Grand Lodge of Virginia. Other colonies soon followed with Delaware, the 13th colony, being the last Provincial Grand Lodge to be formed in 1806.

Colonel Bill Gibson gives further evidence of early military masonic involvement overseas in his article in *Through the Green* entitled 'Golf in New York 1779–1785', where he states that *Long Island has revealed the presence of a substantial number of early military golfers. The 42nd Regiment was stationed in the vicinity of Newtown, (present-*

day Elmhurst, Queens) in 1779. However, they did not receive their lodge warrant until 1811.

The 71st (Highland) Regiment, who participated in the capture of Philadelphia in October 1777, returned to New York shortly afterwards. Their senior officers were Captain Arthur Forbes, Royal Aberdeen Golf Club, Captain Colin Mackenzie, HCEG 1802 and Lieutenant William Nairne, R&A 1782. This regiment received their lodge warrant in 1759.

The 76th (Highland) Regiment arrived in August 1779 together with the 80th Regiment to increase the size of the British armed forces after their defeat at Saratoga in 1777. Both went into captivity with the surrender of Yorktown in October 1781.

The senior officers of the 76th were Lieutenant David Barclay, HCEG 1786, Captain A Montgomery Cunningham, HCEG and Captain Robert McColme, Crail 1790. There is no record of the 76th having a military lodge but there is of the 80th that received their warrant in 1780.

Their senior officers were Captain Alex. Arbuthnott, HCEG 1777, R&A 1783, Captain George Cumine, R&A 1784, Lieutenant James Gibson, HCEG 1787, Major James Gordon, HCEG 1778, Fraserburgh 1778 and Captain David Kinloch, HCEG 1782, R&A 1783.

The American Republic that emerged from the War of Independence was not, in any literal sense, a freemasonic republic, i.e. not a republic created by freemasons for freemasons in accordance with freemasonic ideals.

But it did embody those ideals; it was profoundly influenced by those ideals; and it owed much more to those ideals than is generally recognised or acknowledged.

As one masonic historian has written, Freemasonry has exercised a greater influence upon the establishment and development of this (the American) government than any other single institution. Neither historians nor members of the fraternity since the days of the first Constitutional Conventions have realised how much the United States of America owes to Freemasonry, and how great a part it played in the birth of the nation and the establishment of the landmarks of that civilisation.

It is interesting to note that the American Declaration of Independence embodied many of the ideals and principles of Freemasonry in its text. On issuing the Declaration of Independence, adopted by the Continental Congress on 4 July 1776, the 13 American colonies severed their political connections to Great Britain.

Although many nations accepted the Declaration of Independence, the British Government did not recognise America's independence until the 'Treaty of Paris' in 1783. Under the terms of the Treaty, which also ended the War of American Revolution, Great Britain acknowledged the United States of America as a sovereign and independent nation.

Rev. Neville Barker Cryer in his book 'Delving Beyond the Craft' gives a timeline of the military involvement in Freemasonry overseas emphasising that it was in the developing areas of North America that the military lodges registered their greatest influence.

1751	*British military lodges, mainly affected by Irish traditions, already had their own growing practices regarding knightly Freemasonry and it was this that they would share with their continental counterparts.*
1768	*Albany, New York.*
1769	*References to 14th Regiment of Foot and 29th Regiment of Foot at Boston, USA.*
1780	*Military lodges, which had Irish or Scottish warrants, were practising on the East Coast of America.*
1786	*Amphibious Lodge was warranted at the Marine Barracks, Stonehouse, near Plymouth UK.*
1790	*New York City.*
1801	*Charlestown, South Carolina.*
1845	*Strong military connections to Secret Monitor Degree in Malta.*
1846	*Strong military connections to Secret Monitor Degree in West Indies.*
1848	*Strong military connections to Secret Monitor Degree in Jerusalem.*

It is interesting to note that Thomas Harper, who became a freemason in 1761 before emigrating to the American colonies, was first recorded as a member of an American lodge, the Lodge of Antients No. 190, in Charlestown, South Carolina, in 1774.

On returning to England in 1781 he set himself up as a silversmith in London and was responsible for producing many of the beautiful masonic jewels of that era. He later is recorded as being in the chair for the first meeting of the United Grand Lodge of England on 7 February 1814.

The oldest lodge in the West Indies, founded in Barbados in 1790, is the Albion Lodge No. 196. This is listed under the District Grand Lodge of Barbados and the Eastern Caribbean and includes the islands of Antigua and St Lucia, although John Dickie records in his book 'The Craft' that Parham Lodge of Antigua was formed in 1738.

The 4 Regiment of Foot, who had their own masonic lodge, were garrisoned in Guadeloupe in 1759 and St Lucia in 1778 and may well have had some influence on the spread of Freemasonry in this region of the Caribbean. There were no golf clubs founded on these islands until the 20th century.

The first lodge recorded in Canada was in Halifax, Nova Scotia, in the early 19th Century, around 1820, according to John Dickie in his book entitled 'The Craft'. He also records that the first lodge in Australia was the Australian Social Lodge in Sydney in 1820, however, the first golf club was not founded in Sydney until 1893 so any such connection is unlikely.

In India the first lodges recorded were in Calcutta and Bombay, both in the early 19th Century, and golf clubs were founded in both these cities in 1829 and 1842 respectively, in which Blackheath GC played a major role. The connection between the two disciplines is more than probable.

Rev. Neville Barker Cryer in his book 'I Just Didn't Know That' gives details of an overseas masonic lodge formed in Corfu Town around 1824 during the British rule of 1815–1856 and of another formed in Valetta, Malta in 1805 by English freemasons, namely, the Earl of Moira and Waller Rodwell Wright.

Clearly, by the 19th century, Freemasonry was beginning to make a stronghold in the colonies driven by the presence of the military in these overseas garrisons. In most cases, the construction of golf courses in these colonies came later.

In Europe, however, it was a very different matter. By the 19th Century Freemasonry was well established in France, Italy, Germany, Austria and Spain but, other than France, it had become so politicised that it was condemned by the governments as being subversive and a threat to the interests of their governments. This resulted in Freemasonry being outlawed in these countries and treated as being a destabilising influence causing it to be persecuted and eradicated along with the Jews.

This situation lasted until the 2nd World War, after which Freemasonry became accepted by all except Spain who remained anti-masonic until 2007. In Italy, however, the Pope still governs that Catholics will become excommunicated it they become Masons. Golf did not feature in these countries until the 20th Century; most of their golf clubs were not established until after the 2nd World War.

The expansion of Freemasonry around the globe in the 19th Century was predominantly restricted to the British Empire and its colonies plus the United States of America.

Chapter Ten
The Spread of Golf
Around the World

The spread of golf overseas started at around the same time as Freemasonry, commencing with America. Golf was first played in America between 1795 and 1830 by early Scottish settlers in Charleston, South Carolina, and Savannah, Georgia, but faded away in the early 1800s.

It is claimed that the first golf club and course in America was founded in White Sulphur Springs, West Virginia in 1884, however, the first golf club in the continent of North America was established north of the border in Canada in 1873, namely Royal Montreal Golf Club.

Whilst this may be true, Savannah Golf Club is regarded as the oldest having been formed in 1794. The Savannah Golf Club, as it is known today, was incorporated on 29 December 1899 in Chatham County. The course when laid out embraced a complete line of confederate fortifications that extended across the entire property.

These fortifications are still present to this day. Savannah is believed to be the first American city where the game of golf was played. The date of its founding is well documented in the Club's archives.

David Stirk in his book 'Golf—History and Tradition' states that *perhaps the freemasons' most important effort in encouraging the spread of golf overseas was in introducing the game to America.*

In 1743, David Deas of Charleston, South Carolina, the first Provincial Grand Master Mason in the USA, ordered from Scotland 96 golf clubs and 432 balls, which were sent to him from the port of Leith. David Deas and his brother were from Leith and would have learnt to play golf there.

These clubs and balls were destined to equip a golf club at Charleston and in view of Deas' masonic status would there doubtless have been a masonic lodge.

It would be wrong to claim the establishment of a masonic lodge at Charleston in 1743, although, in the previous chapter, there is a reference to a lodge being in existence at Charleston in 1774. There can only be a likelihood of a lodge being established at this earlier date.

Consignments of equipment were also sent from Glasgow to Virginia and to Maryland for it is recorded by Stirk that in 1750, another 72 golf clubs and 576 feather balls were sent from Glasgow to Virginia and, in 1765, 18 golf clubs and 144 feather balls were sent from Glasgow to Maryland.

Both these consignments relate to golf equipment but there is no mention of a masonic lodge being founded at that time.

Alistair J Johnston and James F Johnston in their 'Chronicles of Golf 1457–1857' expand on the early existence of golf in America when they state that *Dr Benjamin Rush of Philadelphia in 1772 refers to golf being one of his pastimes in a publication produced by John Dunlap, 'Sermons to Gentlemen upon Temperance and Exercise'.*

There is evidence that he lived in Edinburgh for a period that would have exposed him to the traditional Scottish pastime. Consequently, he may have been a pioneer of golf in America. Moreover, his name was to be forever etched in the history of the United States when in 1776 he appended his signature to the Declaration of Independence.

This was also signed by another Scottish emigrant, John Witherspoon, who was a clergyman from Paisley and a friend of Dr Benjamin Rush.

It is recorded in the previous chapter that Freemasonry had already been established in Philadelphia 40 years earlier, a connection between the two cannot be ruled out. Other sporadic attempts to introduce golf into North America were made in Quebec around 1824 but as recorded above, the first golf club established in Canada was the Royal Montreal Golf Club in 1873, where Alexander Dennistoun was the driving force. Quebec Golf Club followed soon after in 1875.

The development of golf in North America was initially slow but it rapidly expanded in the later part of the 19th century. Only three golf clubs were founded in the later part of the 18th century, namely, Charleston 1786, Savannah 1794 and Saroma 1794/95. This remained the same for the next 90 years but in the 10 years after 1884 a further 19 were established, *see* Appendix Two.

The military who were garrisoned in other parts of the world played a similar role. In an article entitled 'Evidence of Golf in Gibraltar' by Neil Millar, William Gibson and David Hamilton, published in *'Through the Green' in* June 2013, they state that in 1773 Richard Twiss recorded golf being played on the sandy spit between Gibraltar and Spain by military officers who were billeted on the island.

At that time there were seven British Regiments stationed in Gibraltar namely: 1st (Royal), 2nd (Queen's Royal), 12th, 39th, 56th, 58th and 69th Regiment of Foot.

Some of the above regiments had military field lodges, namely: 1st, 12th, and 56th and in Chapter Eleven it is recorded that an artillery regiment established a masonic lodge on the island.

The authors of this article have identified six military officers who were most likely to have been playing golf on the sands and had links to Scottish Golf Societies, namely:

Captain James Anstruther of the 58th Regiment of Foot was from Inergelly, Fifeshire in the parish of Kilrenny, nine miles SE of St Andrews. He is recorded as having attended a meeting of the St Andrews Society of Golfers (R&A). He died in December 1776.

Captain James Horsburgh of the 39th Regiment of Foot was elected as a member of the Musselburgh Company of Golfers (Royal Musselburgh Golf Club) in 1784 and subsequently resigned in 1787 after refusing to pay his annual subscription.

Ensign Hamilton Maxwell of the 58th Regiment of Foot, was subsequently promoted to Major in 1778 when he transferred to the 73rd (Highland) Regiment of Foot. He was elected a member of both Leith and St Andrews Societies of Golfers in 1779 and 1783, respectively.

Lieutenant-Colonel Alexander Monypenny of the 56th Regiment of Foot was elected a member of the St Andrews Society of Golfers (R&A) in 1767. He was from Pitmilly, an estate located at Kingbarns, five miles SE of St Andrews.

Lieutenant-Colonel Philip Skene of the 69th Regiment of Foot promoted to Major-General in 1782, was also believed to be a member of the St Andrews Society of Golfers with his father David and his two brothers, Robert and David.

The family home was in Pitlour, Fife, some 20 miles west of St Andrews. Philip bought the Falkland estate in Fife, which was located close to the family home.

Captain John Whyte of the 56th Regiment of Foot, promoted to Lieutenant-Colonel in 1782 when he transferred to the 6th Regiment of Foot, was elected a member of the Gentlemen Golfers of Leith in 1787.

Golf was introduced to the sub-continent of India by soldiers, settlers and government administrators, which resulted in the establishment of Dum Dum Golf Club (Calcutta) in 1830 and Royal Bombay Golf Club in 1842.

However, the Royal Blackheath Golf Club had a significant influence on the foundation of some of the earliest overseas golf clubs by sending them a copy of the Rules of the Blackheath Club to get them started, namely:

Dum Dum Golf Club, nr Calcutta, 1830 (1829).

Bombay Golf Club, 1842

Blackheath Golf Club, New South Wales, 1841

They also sent and received trophies for which each club competes, as recorded by David Stirk in his book, 'Golf—The History of an Obsession' *see* below:

When the Calcutta Golf Club was founded in Dum Dum in 1829 the membership was predominantly Scottish. *Blackheath immediately showed a close interest by toasting the club at one of their dinners. In 1873, they sent a gold medal to the Calcutta Club.*

The Club followed the rules of Blackheath to the letter, including the habit of wearing uniforms and having dinners at which matches were arranged and bets laid on the outcome. Regularly the minutes of the Calcutta Club were, and still are, sent to the parent club at Blackheath.

Blackheath being close to London had a masonic membership derived from the City of London, many of its members were employed by, or were directors of, the East India Company.

Company's employees sent to India kept close links with their masonic brothers at Blackheath Golf Club. It is believed that Blackheath gave a charter to the Calcutta masons to form a lodge in Calcutta and that it should take the form of a golf club similar in constitution to the parent club, Blackheath; their first Captain was made an honorary member of Blackheath Golf Club.

Stirk also records that similar close associations were made with the Bombay Golf Club. Blackheath Golf Club sent them a copy of their rules and a gold medal to be played for in competition. Blackheath had a similar close association with another club in New South Wales, Australia, also called the Blackheath Golf Club.

It is recorded that in 1841, Captain Alex Brodie Spark, who was a Master Mason, sent a gallon of claret to their parent club to celebrate the birth of his son. This generous action led to Alex Brodie Spark being made an honorary member of the parent club.

David Stirk continues, *that freemasons used their considerable influence to spread the game beyond the shores of Britain. Scottish golfing enthusiasts, sent by the great business houses of London or by the Colonial Service to every part of the empire and to other countries, took their game and the love of it with them.*

In addition to Calcutta, Bombay, Montreal and Blackheath, New South Wales, a few golf clubs were formed in the West Indies between 1810 and 1860. Stirk records that in 1810, the Society of Golfers at Blackheath granted a charter and diploma to Charles Mackenzie of Barbados to found a golfing society; the charter was not confirmed until 1817.

In 1814, a similar charter was granted to Charles MacDowell of St Vincent.

Another Colonial example is the Nuwara Eliya Golf Club, Ceylon, which was founded in 1888 as an amenity for the military and colonial officers stationed nearby. This was not the first golf club in Ceylon, that accreditation belongs to Royal Colombo, which was founded in 1882.

A further example of golf being spread around the world is given in an article by Lieutenant-General Sir Robert Richardson entitled 'Golf in South Africa' that was also published in *'Through the Green'*.

December 2013. Sir Robert writes: *The oldest golf club in South Africa was established in 1885 when the Royal Scots (The Royal Regiment) were stationed in Cape Town. Lieutenant-General Samuel Torrens, who commanded the troops in South Africa, played a central role.*

He arrived in Cape Town on 5 November 1885 and formed the Royal Cape Golf Club on 14 November. He recruited 38 playing members and 12 non-players, ordered clubs and balls from John Dunn of North Berwick, where it is believed he was a member, and enlisted a Royal Engineer officer to lay out the 9-hole course.

He was assisted in this venture by Colonel C. C. Daniel who became the first Treasurer and Secretary, whilst Samuel Torrens was the first Captain of the Club and Honorary President. Unfortunately, the Royal Scots were posted to Zululand in July 1888 and did not return but the club survived and is still thriving.

Torrens was subsequently moved on to become the Governor of Malta in 1888, where he established the Royal Malta Golf Club. Another golf club was established in South Africa in 1889, this being the Salisbury Golf Club in Rhodesia, now Zimbabwe, which later became the Royal Harare in 1983.

Bob Fletcher and Richard Williams in their article 'The Oldest Club in the Southern Hemisphere', published in *Through the Green,* September 2019, give a detailed history of the Mauritius Golf Club, which was formed in 1842 following a circular sent out by the Secretary J. A. Anderson to adopt the rules and regulations for playing the game.

The circular went to 33 members and the membership was limited to 40. The 6-hole course was laid out on the *Champ de Mars*, a flat open area east of Port Louis, and measured 900 yds.

This area was formerly used for military exercises during occupation by the French and, following the British conquest, it was laid out as a racecourse. The membership consisted mainly of traders, merchants and professional men with a few Army and Naval officers, who were posted on the island.

The initial club Captain, James Wilson, was the chief justice of the island. Among the military members was Major Sir Robert Douglas, who had command of a reserve battalion of the 12th Regiment of Foot; a Regiment known to have its own military field lodge.

Charles Anderson, who was a member of Montrose Golf Club and the prime mover of the new club in Mauritius, arranged through another Montrose member, Captain Archibald McNeil of the Forfar & Kincardineshire Militia, to send sufficient greenkeeping equipment necessary to construct and maintain the golf course and enough golf equipment for the new members.

Davidson, the Montrose club-maker, exported further golf clubs and balls to Mauritius in 1844.

Their dining after golf took part in one of the local hotels. They wore scarlet waistcoats with gold buttons and toasts were drunk to *the health of brother golfers in their native land*. The word *brother* suggests that there may have been a masonic link. The arranging of matches and the making of bets was also part of their custom at these dinners.

The Club's patron was General Sir William Gomm, who was the Governor of the Colony. The Club ceased to exist in the 1850s most probably following the island's cholera epidemic in 1854.

Fletcher and Williams also researched another Mauritian Golf Club in a later article entitled 'Early Golf in Mauritius', also published in *Through the Green*, March 2020. The Club is currently known as the Gymkhana Club, but its name and history have had many changes over the years.

The precise date of its formation is a record vague but there is in 1849 to provide recreational and sporting facilities to officers of HM Armed Forces. The Club was named the Mauritius Military Gymkhana Club at Vacoas, which is in the centre of the island.

After the British took occupation of the island in 1810, a large military garrison was established on the coast consisting of two battalions of the 12th and 35th Regiments of Foot and two Indian battalions. These were later relocated to Curepipe, which is southeast of Vacoas; the administrative HQ was located at Vacoas. The 12th Regiment of Foot had a masonic lodge, *see* Appendix Four.

The facilities consisted of a polo ground with a 6-hole golf course laid out around its perimeter. When polo was abandoned during the 1st World War, the course was extended to 9-holes.

The Club was renamed the Naval and Military Gymkhana Club after the last serving battalion left the island in the 1950s and was handed over to the Royal Navy, who had established a radio transmission station on the island.

The loss of the military presence meant that the number of servicemen on the island was now considerably diminished, and many civilians were invited to become members.

The Club was finally handed over to the islanders in 1976, eight years after independence and renamed the Gymkhana Club. The Club is still in existence today and is now a full 18-hole course with a local membership of 500.

It was during this period of expansion that in 1856, the British founded the first golf club in mainland Europe at Pau, in the foothills of the Pyrenees. It was maintained by Stirk that Blackheath Golf Club had close connections with this club and all the early golf clubs founded in India.

The development of golf in Europe did not progress at the same speed as the colonies, the Royal Antwerp Golf Club in Belgium was founded in 1888, but it was not until 1899 that the Royal Homburger Golf Club was established in Germany. It is the third oldest club in the country and is in the spa town of Bad Homburg.

Its Royal prefix came as a result of the long-standing relationship of our own Royal Family, specifically the Prince of Wales, later King Edward VII, who spent much time in this town. The right to use the *Royal* prefix was approved by Queen Elizabeth II in 2013.

The course was laid out and the Club was founded completely on an English initiative, as a direct result of the long-standing relationship of the town with the British Royal Family. The Club's first President was Field Marshall, HRH Prince George Duke of Cambridge, a cousin to Queen Victoria.

There can be no doubt that in the early years, the military had a very significant impact on the foundation of golf clubs in the colonies and elsewhere around the world.

Chapter Eleven
The Military Connection
The Conduit

The values and standards of the British Army are known as *loyalty, integrity and co-operation* and these fit snugly with the principles of Freemasonry and it is no wonder that Freemasonry plays such an important role in the military.

The extent of the involvement of the military with Freemasonry, even in the early years, is well documented by Brig. P R Sharpe in his article *'A Short History of the Armed Forces and Masonry'*, published on the website of Military Masons.

In this article, he attempts to summarise the connection between the British Military and British Freemasonry during the formative years of both, this being 1700–1900. During this period the British Empire rose to its zenith and Freemasonry developed into what is regarded today as speculative masonry.

It is maintained by Sharpe that *the army is considered pivotal during this period and had the greatest part to play in the expansion of Freemasonry. The 18th century saw the re-*

establishment of a standing army after the nation almost disbanded land forces post the English civil war.

This caused a rapid reversal of policy dictated by parliament and resulted in the formation of Life, Foot and Dragoon Guards who were utterly loyal to the monarch.

He continues, that *the war of the Spanish Succession (1702–1713) saw the first real test abroad of the post-civil war army. The rise of John Churchill to become the Duke of Marlborough and his four great victories of Blenheim, Ramilies, Oudenard and Malplaquet established the British Army as a major force in Europe.*

The expansion of British interests in its fledgling colonies also became a major focus for military activity. America, India and the West Indies began to call for garrisons of substantial troops.

These continental and colonial commitments began to shape the British Army, which found itself involved in the Seven Years' War. This led to theatres of operation in Europe, North America and India.

The Seven Years' War (1756–1763) resulted in the expansion of British interests in Canada, India and the West Indies with St Lucia, Grenada and Florida being transferred to British territories in the post-war treaty.

However, 11 years later the British Army found itself embroiled in the American War of Independence, which significantly dented the confidence of both the nation and its army.

Throughout the 19th century, the army continued to expand the existing colonies and now turned its attention to

Africa, i.e. South Africa, North and South Rhodesia, Tanganyika, Kenya, Egypt and the Sudan. The century ended with the Zulu and Boer Wars where the use of modern weaponry was introduced.

These ultimately had such a devastating effect on the Great War. Prior to that the lessons learnt from the Crimean War led to a top-to-bottom reform of the army in 1868 by Edward Cardwell, the Secretary of State for War.

Sharpe considers that *it was the regimental system during those 200 years that formed the basis of the formation of military masonic lodges. From 1751 all regiments were ranked in order of precedence, i.e. 1st, 2nd, to the 103rd of Foot.*

This same system was applied to the cavalry. However, the militia and Fencible Regiments were named after the County where they were based.

Much has been written about the Knights Templars and their link with Freemasonry although there is no direct association with the order. The Templars were a powerful military order, feared by their adversaries in combat and respected for their skills in building castles and churches.

Sharpe considers them to be responsible for the start of the Gothic period in Europe. They were also recognised for their financial acumen, operating the world's first Bank, which brought them wealth and with it so much power as to be seen as a threat to the monarchy in France.

This ultimately resulted in their arrest on Friday 13th 1307 with subsequent torture and death. Following this, their assets were seized and the order was outlawed, but many managed to escape to Scotland where they settled and maintained their traditions and culture plus, it is believed, their wealth, but this has never been proven.

Their presence in Scotland is most evident in the carvings found in the Rosslyn Chapel, which is dated around 1440 and is located just outside Edinburgh.

Some of the carvings depict an initiation ceremony showing a hoodwinked candidate dressed in a Knights Templar uniform with a cable tow about his neck. Others relate to other masonic symbols.

Brig P R Sharpe suggests there is evidence that *the first senior military figures to become a mason were General Sir Alexander Hamilton and the Quartermaster General— General Sir Robert Moray.*

They were received into the Edinburgh Lodge No. 1, Scottish Constitution in 1641 and, although Scottish soldiers, it took place on English soil at Newcastle-upon-Tyne.

In the early years, as recorded above, there were initially three Grand Lodges, Scotland, England and Ireland, all operating as separate constitutions. At this time, military lodges found difficulty in obtaining warrants from the Scottish and English constitutions.

Consequently, many of them applied to the Irish Grand Lodge which willingly accepted them. The military lodges created under the Irish Constitution are listed by Sharpe as: *The 1st of Foot (Royal Scots) petitioned the Grand Lodge of Ireland in 1732 and became the first regiment to gain warrant No. 11, which was dated 7th November of that year.*

This opened the floodgates and over the next 10 years, Irish warrants were granted to the following Regiments of

Foot: 17th (Leicestershire), 18th (Royal Irish), 19th (Green Howards), 20th (Lancashire Fusiliers), 27th (Royal Inniskilling Fusiliers), 28th (Gloucestershire), 30th (South Staffords) and the 39th (Dorset).

It was not until 1747, that the Grand Lodge of Scotland commenced issuing military warrants. These were given to the 12th Suffolk, 55th (2nd Border) and 2nd Scots Greys, which was a cavalry regiment. In 1755, the 57th of Foot (Middlesex) was issued the first ancient warrant.

After this date warrants were issued to all branches of the armed services by the three Grand Lodges. Sharpe records that in all 581 ambulatory warrants have been issued, including four to ship companies. The Royal Marines, however, are in immovable garrisons and are consequently issued with permanent warrants.

One of the four naval warrants was issued to HMS Vanguard. Thomas Dunkerley was HMS Vanguard's Master Gunner and an illegitimate son of George II. He was given the authority from the Premier Grand Lodge to grant warrants and duly installed the first Provincial Grand Master of Canada at Quebec.

The future of field lodges was unpredictable as the regiments that were periodically garrisoned abroad took their ambulatory warrants with them but when they were garrisoned overseas for long periods they surrendered their travelling warrants and set up an immoveable lodge under the jurisdiction of the Province in which they were garrisoned.

Many of the ambulatory warrants became casualties of war, dictated by the fortunes of battle and the loss of lodge members.

It was during this period that, as the empire expanded, military lodges expanded likewise taking with them their ambulatory warrants and many overseas masonic temples can be traced back to these regiments. Sharpe informs us that artillery lodges were established in Gibraltar, Canada and India.

He also advised that the 46th of Foot after 95 years of travelling, finally settled in Canada and became Lodge No. 1 of the Grand Lodge of Quebec. A similar situation exists in Sydney, Australia, where another Irish military lodge is now the Australian Social Lodge No. 1 of New South Wales.

The spread of Freemasonry throughout the globe was encouraged by colonial regiments and their British officers, establishing lodges under the Irish and Scottish constitutions.

Although most have now disappeared, their historical presence remains such as the Bermuda Garrison Lodge No. 580 in the West Indies, as well as others in Pakistan, Zambia, Kenya and South Africa.

The most notable example of this occurs in New York where three Antient lodges were joined by three travelling lodges, one Irish, one Scottish and one other.

This led in 1781 to the Antient Grand Lodge of England warranting a Provincial Grand Lodge of New York No. 219, which in 1784, after nine months of independence, became the Grand Lodge of America.

Appendix Six lists a number of military masonic heroes who relate to the findings of P R Sharpe.

The above certainly establishes the direct involvement of Freemasonry in the military from the 1700s, which was largely practised by the officers in a number of the regiments; the lower ranks not being admitted until much later.

During this period, there were also several officers who were military golfers, and it is not inconceivable that many of them were freemasons as well. A number of these military golfers are listed in an article published in *'Through the Green'*, June 2015, entitled 'Military Golfers in the Waterloo Campaign' by Col. William H Gibson and they are as follows:

Lt. Col Robert Macara, *42nd (Blackwatch) Regt.* A member of Royal Blackheath Golf Club 1796–1799; became a member of R&A 1810 and two months later, appears in the minute book of Royal Musselburgh Golf Club 1810 and 1811. He died during the Battle of Waterloo in 1815.

Maj. Robert Henry Dick, *42nd (Blackwatch) Regt.* a member of the R&A. Promoted to Major-General in the Madras Army and killed in the Battle of Sobroan, Punjab, 1846.

Bt. Maj. John Campbell, *42nd (Blackwatch) Regt.* he is recorded in the minute book of Royal Musselburgh Golf Club as playing at the club in 1811.

Capt. Archibald Menzies, *42nd (Blackwatch) Regt.* he is recorded in the minute book of Royal Musselburgh Golf Club that he was present at the club in 1811. He was injured in the Battle at Quatre Bras in 1815.

Prince Frederick Duke of Brunswick-Wolfenbutel, *Brunswick Corps* is recorded as playing at Royal Blackheath Golf Club in 1812 and again in 1813. Died at the battle at Quatre Bras in 1815.

Capt. David Baird, *3rd (Scots Fusilier) Guards* was elected a member of R&A 1812 and Captain of the R&A in 1843. He was a founder member and the first Captain of North Berwick Golf Club in 1832.

Capt. Robert Bruce, *1st (Grenadier Guards)* a member of R&A 1814, Captain of R&A in 1819 and a member of North Berwick Golf Club from 1833.

Capt. William F Browne, *6th Inniskilling Dragoons* a founder member of North Berwick Golf Club in 1832.

Capt. Robert Boyle, *42nd (Blackwatch) Regt.* was a member of the Royal Musselburgh Golf Club in 1814, when his regiment played at the club. He died in 1821.

Capt. Daniel McIntosh, *42nd (Blackwatch) Regt.* was recorded as an Hon. Member of Royal Musselburgh in 1811.

Quartermaster Donald McIntosh, *42nd (Blackwatch) Regt.* was a founding member of the Royal Perth Golfing Society in 1824. The Royal prefix was granted in 1833.

There is ample evidence of the presence of Freemasonry in the British Army and of their masonic influence around the world. There is also a direct link between the officers of the various regiments and early golf clubs and golf societies.

Trying to relate all three is an impossible task without documentary evidence of the names of the founder members of those clubs and societies. Sadly, most of their early records seem to have been lost or destroyed. It can therefore only be conjectured that such a link exists.

Chapter Twelve
Summary

John Acaster, who was a Senior Warden of the *Quatuor Coronati* Lodge No. 2076, expressed his opinion that *It certainly seems that golf clubs have often been started by and/or warmly supported by freemasons. But that is nothing to do with anything symbolic or esoteric. It is purely from a combination of circumstances that,*

   a) *freemasons have often been quite wealthy and well-connected.*
   b) *they tend to be or become vibrant social animals; and*
   c) *the pleasures of jocundity, the bar and the table tend to be engrained. It may be that such close acquaintance and talk may have been helpful in commercial terms, as might be expected, but that would not be the driver (so to speak) for a 9 or 18-hole foundation (of a golf course).*

John Acaster further confirmed the belief that the spread of golf with Freemasonry across the empire is justified. The *Quatuor Coronati* Lodge is a vehicle for delivering research papers on the history of Freemasonry that are published in their bulletins.

It is hoped that the research contained in this text has established a significant link between the growth of Freemasonry and the foundation of golf clubs. Furthermore, ably assisted by the militia, there is evidence that both share a responsibility for the establishment of golf clubs around the world.

Whilst the findings of this research have been unable to establish a direct link between golf and Freemasonry during those formative years, they were both practised and engaged in by gentlemen of the same social strata and inevitably an indirect link is indisputable.

It is hoped that in time further evidence may be uncovered that will give a clearer picture, but that will be for someone else to research. My quest, for now, is over.

David L Dobby January 2025

Appendices

Appendix One
Earliest Golf Clubs in UK

The following list is in date order of the earliest known existence of golf clubs in the United Kingdom of which the first 36 were contacted in my research in relation to any masonic connections with the formation of their club, plus 3 other golf clubs; 20 of the 36 responded plus the 3 others.

I am most grateful to those who responded to my enquiries, they have all helped in drawing a picture of the social circumstances prevailing in those early years. But it was disappointing that the other 16 failed to respond.

Whilst this research is not comprehensive the answers received give an indication of the relationship between Freemasonry and golfers during each club's formative period.

1562	**Montrose Links**, Angus
	Information received from Alan Crow in the form of *'Golf in Montrose'* by William Coull.
1608	**Royal Blackheath**, Kent Some details obtained from David Stirk's book *'Golf—the History of an Obsession'* and the club history, *'Four Hundred Years of the Blackheath Golfer'*.

1735	**Royal Burgess Golfing Society of Edinburgh,** Midlothian. Response negative but a further response included with Bruntsfield Links Golf Society.
1744	**Hon. Co. of Edinburgh Golfers,** East Lothian An article entitled *'Leith to Muirfield via Musselburgh'* published in *Through the Green*, Sept 2013, by Bobby Burt covers most of the relevant history,
1754	**Royal & Ancient,** Fife Response received from Angela Howe, Director of Museum & Heritage suggesting that I should refer to Alistair Johnston's chapter on the subject in his *Chronicles of Golf*.
1761	**Bruntsfield Links Golfing Society**, Midlothian Information received from Pat Colledge enclosing a page from David Hamilton's book *'Golf— Scotland's Game'* together with a chapter from the History of Bruntsfield Links entitled *'The Missing Minute Book'*. Reference was also made to David Stirk's book *'Golf—History and Tradition'*. Pat also suggested that masonic members were supporters of the king, whereas Jacobites were for Bonnie Prince Charlie.
1762	**Bray,** Co. Wicklow, Eire Details obtained from an article entitled *'The First Golf Club in Ireland'*, published in *'Through the Green'*, Sept 2012.
1774	**Royal Musselburgh**, East Lothian Alistair Davie, Secretary of the club and WM of Thorntree Lodge rang to advise that Royal Musselburgh has masonic connections and so does Thorntree Golf Club and he will make enquiries on my behalf. He also believed that there was a military connection. Furthermore, he was to make enquiries from the Grand Lodge of Scotland on the subject

	before coming back to me. Sadly, no further information has been received.
1780	**Royal Aberdeen**, Aberdeenshire Information received from James Christie, but they have no connections with Freemasonry.
1786	**Crail Golfing Society**, Fife No response
1787	**Glasgow, Glasgow** Useful information received from Nevin McGhee, who Referred me to his article *'Anent the Golf'* published in *Through the Green*, Sept 2013.
1797	**Burntisland** (Club), Fife No response
1817	**St Andrews Thistle** (Club), Fife No response
1817	**Scotscraig**, Fife No response
1810	**Royal Montrose,** Angus No response
1818	**Old Manchester (Club),** Manchester Graham Waters advised that he was not aware of Freemasonry being involved although the military were barracked in the vicinity, camping on Kersal Moor. Names of founder members supplied.
1820	**Leven Golfing Society,** Fife Archie Shanks advised on the various club structures at Leven but there is no masonic connection to his knowledge.
1824	**Royal Perth Golfing Society** (Club), Perthshire No masonic connection.
1832	**North Berwick**, East Lothian None known but further enquiries were being made. Sadly, none received.
1841	**Peterhead**, Aberdeenshire Response received from John Arthur. He suggested contact with Neil Masson but no response has been received regarding founder members or masonic members.
1842	**Carnoustie,** Angus Alex Mackenzie advised no masonic connection.

1843	**St Andrews** (Club), Fife No Response
1845	**Panmure**, Angus No response
1846	**Leven Club**, Fife No response
1851	**Lanark**, Lanark's Response received referring to their website for their connection to the militia. Details extracted from the club's history concerning the influence of the militia, naming the Regiments concerned.
1851	**Prestwick**, Ayrshire Andrew Lochhead (Club Archivist) is not aware of any such connection. The names of some of the founder members received.
1851	**Prestwick St Nicholas**, Ayrshire No response
1853	**Portobello**, Midlothian Response received from Czeslaw Kruk giving details of a masonic connection and masonic lodges attached to the club.
1853	**Tantallon** (Club), East Lothian No response
1854	**Dirleton Castle**, East Lothian Response received but no masonic connection.
1855	**Cupar**, Fife No response
1856	**Dunbar,** East Lothian Information on the Dunbar Golfing Society received from John Harris confirming a close association with Freemasonry and some of its members.
1856	**Thorntree** (Club), East Lothian Details to be provided by Royal Musselburgh but, sadly, none received.
1858	**King James VI,** Perthshire Initial response received, no masonic connection.
1858	**The Curragh, Ireland** Details obtained from an article by Col William Gibson published in *'Through the Green'*, June 2011.
1860	**Girvan,** Ayrshire
1865	Haddington, East Lothian

1865	London Scottish, Surrey
1965	**Royal Wimbledon,** Surrey Response received and details provided by club member, Hugh Grieve.
1867	Kilspindie, East Lothian
1867	Leven Thistle, Fife
1868	Dalhousie, Angus
1868	Lundin, Fife
1869	Alnmouth, Northumberland
1869	Alnmouth Village, Northumberland
1869	Royal Liverpool, Merseyside
1869	Stirling, Stirlingshire
1870	Wick, Caithness & Sutherland
1871	Forfar, Angus
1872	Furness, Cumbria
1873	Bass Rock (Club), East Lothians
1873	Carnoustie Ladies, Angus
1873	Newbury & Crookham, Berks
1873	Royal West Lancashire, Merseyside
1874	Seaton Carew, Durham
1875	Golf House Club, Fife
1875	Muir of Ord, Caithness & Sutherland
1875	Pontnewydd, Monmouthshire
1875	Southfield-Oxfordshire
1876	Machrihanish, Argyll & Bute
1877	Airdrie, Lanarks
1877	Hawick, Borders
1877	Haydock Park, Merseyside
1877	Longridge, Lancs
1877	Royal Dornoch, Caithness & Sutherland
1878	Royal Troon, Ayrshire
1879	Ladybank, Fife
1880	Alexandra Park, Glasgow
1880	Ardeer, Ayrshire

1880	Bath, Somerset
1880	Bramshaw, Hants
1880	Dumfries & Galloway, D & G
1880	Felixstowe Ferry, Suffolk
1880	Kingsdown, Wilts
1880	Melrose, Borders
1881	Fraserburgh, Aberdeenshire
1881	Royal Belfast, Co Down
1883	Army, Hants
1893	**Chislehurst,** Kent Martyn Start sent the history of Camden Place Lodge that was formed 10 years after the golf club. Peter Stevenson has also sent the history of Chislehurst Golf Club that relates to this Lodge.
1903	**Shooter's Hill,** London Response received giving details of a masonic connection and its relation to Clapham Common Golf Club.

Appendix Two
Earliest Overseas Golf Clubs

Current records suggest that the Savannah Golf Club is not the earliest recorded in the USA, they are the following:

1786	Charleston, South Carolina	USA
1794	Savannah, Georgia	USA
1794/95	Saroma, South Carolina	USA
1884	White Sulphur Springs West Virginia	USA
1884	Edgewood, Tivoli, New York	USA
1887	Quogue Field, New York	USA
1887	Foxburg CC, Pennsylvania	USA
1887	Essex County CC, New Jersey	USA
1888	Kebo Valley, Maine	USA
1891	Shinnecock Hills, New York	USA
1892	Oakhurst, West Virginia	USA
1892	Palmetto, South Carolina	USA
1892	Glen Arven, Thomasville, Georgia	USA
1893	Newport CC, Rhode Island	USA
1893	Chicago	USA
1893	Victoria, Mississippi	USA
1893	Segregansett, Taunton, Mass.	USA
1894	Otsego, New York	USA

1894	Tacoma, Washington	USA

Elsewhere the earliest golf clubs recorded are as follows:

1829	Royal Calcutta	India
1841	Blackheath, New South Wales	Australia
1842	Bombay	India
1842	Mauritius	Mauritius
1849	Gymkhana Club	Mauritius
1856	Pau	France
1870	Royal Adelaide	Australia
1871	Otago	New Zealand
1873	Christchurch	New Zealand
1873	Royal Montreal	Canada
1874	Royal Quebec	Canada
1876	Toronto	Canada
1878	Buenos Aires	Argentina
1882	Royal Colombo	Ceylon
1884	Nuwara Eliya	Ceylon
1885	Royal Cape	South Africa
1888	Karachi, Sindh	India
1888	Royal Malta	Malta
1888	Royal Antwerp	Belgium
1889	Royal Hong Kong	Hong Kong
1889	Royal Harare (Salisbury)	Zimbabwe
1890	San Paulo	Brazil
1890	Royal Queensland	Australia
1891	Royal Melbourne	Australia
1891	Cannes	France
1893	Royal Sydney	Australia
1895	Royal Perth	Australia
1895	Istanbul	Turkey
1899	Royal Homburger	Germany
1900	Royal Hobart	Tasmania.

Appendix Three
Military Field Lodges
Prior to 1860

Lodge No.	Date of Warrant	Current Status	Name of Lodge and Regiment
	1743	Erased	Pittsford—55th Regiment of Foot. Regiment disbanded 1748
58	1747	E1806	Duke of Norfolk's—12th Duke of Norfolk Regiment of Foot (Royal Anglian Reg.)
63	1751 1763	Lost	The Mason's—Gen. Husk's Reg. 23rd replaced by Reg. of Foot (Royal Welch Fusiliers)
137	1767	E1816	
73	1754	E1809	White's—32nd Reg. of Foot (The Light Infantry)
79	1760	E1852	Fort George—31st Reg. of Foot (The Queen's Regiment)

92	1759	E1809	Prince of Wales from Edinburgh—71st Reg. of Foot (Royal Highland Fusiliers) [Princess Margaret's Own Guard]
97	1759	E1809	Hooker St John—70th Reg. of Foot (The Queen's Regiment)
101	1760	E1809	King George III—56th (Pompadours) Regiment of Foot (Royal Anglian Reg.)
106	1761	E1816	Duke of York's—64th Reg. of Foot
108	1761	E1816	St George's—31st Reg. of Foot (The Queen's Regiment)
121	1764	E1809	Union—94th Reg. of Foot (The Scots USA Brigade, Holland)
132	1767	E1809	Lodge Mariah—22nd Reg. of Foot (The New York Cheshires)
147	1769	E1809	United—4th Reg. of Foot (The King's Own Royal Border Reg.)
156	1769	E1816	St Patrick's—43rd Reg. of Foot (The Quebec Royal Greenjackets)
158	1763		Royal Scots Greys Kilwinning—Royal Reg. of Scots Dragoons

Reissued	1770	E1816	St Andrews Royal Arch—Royal North British Dragoons (the Royal Scots Greys) [the Royal Scots Dragoon Guards]
159	1785	E1853	Royal Arch Union—3rd Reg. of Dragoons (The Queen's Own Hussars)
168	1771	E1816	Lodge Unity—17th Reg. of Foot (The Nova Scotia Royal Anglian Reg.)
188	1776	E1816	Queen's—7th Dragoons (Queen's) [The Queen's Own Hussars]
197	1780	E1785	St Andrew—80th Reg. of Foot (Royal Edinburgh Volunteers 1778–84)
207	1799	E1837	Aboyne 6th North British Militia—6th Battalion North British Militia
213	1806	E1848	Orange—51st Reg. of Foot (the Royal Scots) [The Royal Reg.]
222	1835	E1852	Royal Lodge Thistle—1st Reg. of Foot Quebec (the Royal Scots) [The Royal Regiment]
225	1808	Current	Lodge of Forfar & Kincardine—Forfar & Kincardine Militia but civilian lodge since 1815

239	1811	E1848	St Andrew—42nd (The Royal Highland) Reg. of Foot (The Black Watch) [Royal Highland]
258	1795	E1809	Argyllshire Military St John—Argyllshire Fencible Regiment
260	1796	E1816	Union Royal Arch—3rd (King's Own Hussars) Reg. of Dragoons (The Queen's Own Hussars)
271	1799		Ayr & Renfrew Militia St Paul—Ayr & Renfrew Militia—Regiment disbanded
	1802		New warrant
204		current	Ayr St Paul—civilian lodge
280	1808	E1852	Lodge Royal Thistle—1st Reg. of Foot (The Quebec Royal Scots) [The Royal Regiment]
320	1813	E1848	St Cuthbert—Durham Militia
328	1830	E1860	George William—94th Reg. of Foot (The Connaught Rangers-disbanded 1921)
373	1856	E1864	Star in the East Turkish contingent to the Crimea (at Kerch)

Details extracted from *History of British & Colonial Regiments and their Military Lodges Vol. 1 Parts 1 and 2.*

Appendix Four
List of Regiments with Masonic Lodges

1st (Royal) Regiment of Foot 1751–1812

Raised 28 March 1633 in Scotland for French service.
Was an English Establishment in 1661 and in 1666–67; permanently from 1678.

1st Regiment of Foot (Royal Scots) 1812–1821
1st or Royal Regiment of Foot 1821–1871
1st or Royal Scots Regiment of Foot 1871–1881

1881: Lothian Regiment (Royal Scots).
2012: Royal Regiment of Scotland.

4th (The King's Own) Regiment of Foot 1751–1867

Raised 13 July 1680 as the 2nd Tangier Regiment.

4th (The King's Own Royal) Regiment of Foot 1867–1881

1881: The King's Own Royal Regiment (Lancaster).
2012: Duke of Lancaster's Regiment.

12th Regiment of Foot 1751–1782

Raised 20 June 1685 as the Duke of Norfolk's Regiment of Foot.

12th (East Suffolk) Regiment of Foot 1782–1881

1881: The Suffolk Regiment.
2012: Royal Anglian Regiment.

17th Regiment of Foot 1751–1782

Raised 27 September 1688 as Soloman Richard's Regiment of Foot.

17th (Leicestershire) Regiment of Foot 1782–1881

1881: The Leicestershire Regiment
2012: Royal Anglian Regiment

22nd Regiment of Foot 1751–1782

Raised 8 March 1689 as the Duke of Norfolk's Regiment of Foot.

22nd (Cheshire) Regiment of Foot 1782–1881

1881: The Cheshire Regiment.
2012: Mercian Regiment.

23rd (Royal Welsh Fusiliers) Regiment of Foot 1751–1881

Raised 16 March 1689 as Lord Herbert's Regiment of Foot.
1881: Royal Welsh Fusiliers.
2012: Royal Welsh Regiment

31st Regiment of Foot 1751–1782

Reraised 14 April 1702 as George Villiers's Regiment of Marines.
Converted to line infantry 1714.

31st (Huntingdonshire) Regiment of Foot 1782–1881

1881: 1st Battalion the East Surrey Regiment.
2012: The Princess of Wales's Royal Regiment.

32nd Regiment of Foot 1751–1782

Raised 12 February 1702 as Edward Fox's Regiment of Marines.
Converted to line infantry in 1715.

32nd (Cornwall) Regiment of Foot 1782–1858
32nd (Cornwall) Light Infantry 1858–1881

1881: 1st Battalion the Duke of Cornwall's Light Infantry
2012: The Rifles

42nd Regiment of Foot 1751–1758
42nd (The Royal Highland) Regiment of Foot 1758–1861

Six independent Highland Companies were raised on 24 April 1725.

The Earl of Craufurd's Regiment was formed on 25 October 1739 by the regimentation of the independent companies. Ranked as 43rd Foot in 1747, renumbered to 42nd in 1749 on disbanding of existing 42nd regiment.

Known as the Highland Regiment.

42nd (The Royal Highland) Regiment of Foot (The Black Watch) 1861–1881

1881: 1st Battalion, the Black Watch (Royal Highlanders).

2012: Royal Regiment of Scotland

43rd Regiment of Foot 1751–1782
43rd (Monmouthshire) Regiment of Foot 1782–1803

Raised 1 March 1741 as Thomas Fowke's Regiment of Foot, ranked as 54th Foot in 1747.

43rd (Monmouthshire Light Infantry) Regiment of Foot

1881: 1st Battalion, the Oxfordshire Light Infantry.
2012: The Rifles

51st Regiment of Foot (8th Marines) 1739–1748

Raised in 1740 as William Hanmer's Regiment of Marines, disbanded in 1748.

51st Regiment of Foot (Cape Breton Regiment) 1754–1756.

Raised in New England in 1754 and disbanded in 1756.

51st Regiment of Foot 1757–1782
51st (2nd York, West Riding) Regiment of Foot 1782–1809

Raised as 53rd Regiment of Foot 1755, renumbered in 1757 on disbandment of existing 50th and 51st Foot.

1881: 1st Battalion, the king's own Light Infantry (South Yorkshire Regiment)

2012: The Rifles.

56th Regiment of Foot 1741–1748

Raised 11 January 1741 as Daniel Houghton's Regiment of Foot.

Ranked 56th, it was renumbered 45th in 1748 on disbandment of 10 regiments of marines.

56th Regiment of Foot 1755–1757

Raised in 1755 as the 58th Regiment of Foot, renumbered 54th in 1757 on disbandment of the existing 50th and 51st Foot.

56th Regiment of Foot 1757–1782
56th (West Essex) Regiment of Foot 1782–1881

Raised in 1755 as the 58th Regiment of Foot, renumbered as 56th in 1757 on disbandment of existing 50th and 51st Foot.

1881: 2nd Battalion, the Essex Regiment
2012: The Royal Anglian Regiment.

64th Regiment of Foot 1745–1748

Raised 1745 as Earl of Loudoun's regiment, disbanded 1748.

64th Regiment of Foot 1757–1758

Raised in 1757 and renumbered 79th Foot in 1758 when second battalions of several regiments raised in 1756 were constituted as 61st to 75th Regiment of Foot.

64th Regiment of Foot 1758–1782
64th (2nd Staffordshire) Regiment of Foot 1782–1881

raised as 2nd Battalion, 11th Regiment of Foot 1756, reconstituted as 64th Regiment of Foot 1758.

1881: The Prince of Wales's (North Staffordshire Regiment)
2012: The Mercian Regiment

70th Regiment of Foot 1758–1782
70th (Surrey) Regiment of Foot 1782–1812

70th (Glasgow Lowland) Regiment of Foot 1812–1825
70th (Surrey) Regiment of Foot 1825–1881

Raised as 2nd Battalion, 31st Regiment of Foot 1756, reconstituted as 70th Regiment of Foot 1758
1881: 2nd Battalion, the East Surrey Regiment.
2012: The Princess of Wales's Royal Regiment.

71st Regiment of Foot 1758–1763

raised as 2nd Battalion, 32nd Regiment of Foot, reconstituted as 71st Regiment of Foot 1758. Disbanded 1763.

71st Regiment of Foot 1764–1769

Raised in 1757 as the 81st (Invalids) Regiment of Foot, renumbered 71st in 1764 following disbandment of a number of senior regiments.
Dispersed to independent garrison companies in 1768/69.

71st (Highland) Regiment of Foot 1775–1786

Raised October 1775 in the Scottish Highlands for service in North America.
Disbanded 1786.

71st (Glasgow Highland) Regiment of Foot 1808–1809
71st (Highland Light Infantry) Regiment of Foot 1810–1881

Formed as 73rd (Highland) Regiment of Foot 1777 by regimentation of independent companies raised in 1771, renumbered as 71st in 1786 on disbandment of existing 71st and 72nd Foot.

1881: 1st Battalion, the Highland Light Infantry.
2012: Royal Regiment of Scotland.

80th (Light Armed) Regiment of Foot 1758–1764

Raised in 1758, disbanded in 1764.

80th (Royal Edinburgh Volunteers) Regiment of Foot 1778–1784

Raised 1778, disbanded 1784.

80th (Staffordshire Volunteers) Regiment of Foot 1778–1784

Raised in 1793 from the Staffordshire Militia.
1881: 2nd Battalion, South Staffordshire Regiment
2012: Mercian Regiment

94th Regiment of Foot (Royal Welsh Volunteers) 1760–1763

Raised in 1760 for service in North America. Disbanded 1763.

94th Regiment of Foot 1780–1783 was raised in 1780 and disbanded in 1783.

94th (Irish) Regiment of Foot 1794–1796 was raised in 1794 and disbanded in 1796.

94th (Scots Brigade) Regiment of Foot 1802–1818

Scotch Brigade was raised for Dutch service in 1568, and placed on the British establishment in 1794. numbered in 1802. Disbanded in 1818.

94th Regiment of Foot 1823–1881 was raised in 1823. In 1875 it was deemed to be the successor of 94th Foot of 1802–1818.
1881: 2nd Battalion, the Connaught Rangers disbanded 1922.

Regiment of Royal Scots Greys (2nd Dragoons) 1678–1971

Royal North British Dragoons (Royal Scots Greys)
The Royal Scots Dragoon Guards

Regiment of 3rd Dragoon Guards (Prince of Wales) 1685–1922

3rd King's Own Hussars 1685–1958
3rd Caroliniers (Prince of Wales's Dragoon Guards) 1922–1971

Regiment of 7th Dragoons

7th Queen's Own Hussars 1689–1958
The Queen's

Durham Militia 1759–1816

Formed in 1759 and led by Henry Vane, 2nd Earl of Darlington
First bandmaster was William Herchel
They were stationed in Musselburgh in 1812, Perth in 1813 and Glasgow in 1814.
Disbanded in 1816.

21st (Royal British Fusilier) Regiment of Foot (1713–1877)

Fought against Jacobites at the Battle of Culloden in April 1746 during the Second Jacobite Rebellion. Numbered 21st Regiment in 1751.

Forfar and Kincardine Militia

Raised in 1798 as the Forfarshire Militia
1802 became the Forfar and Kincardine Militia until 1854 when it was re-designated the Forfar and Kincardine Artillery.
1902 renamed Forfar and Kincardine Royal Garrison Artillery (Militia)
It was disbanded in 1909.

2nd Argyllshire (Fencible) Regiment 1794–1802

Raised October 1794 under Colonel Henry Mord Clavering.
Served in Ireland and was disbanded in 1802 at Ayr.

Appendix Five
Overseas Posting of Regiments with Military Lodges Prior to 1860

1st Regiment of Foot (Royal Scots)
Royal Lodge Thistle No. 222, 1835–1852

1830	Scotland
1836	Canada
1843	West Indies
1846	Scotland

4th Regiment of Foot (King's Own Border Regiment)
The United Lodge No. 147, 1769–1809

1759	West Indies	Guadeloupe
1778	West Indies	St Lucia

12th Duke of Norfolk's Regiment of Foot
The Duke of Norfolk's Lodge No. 58, 1747–1806

No details

17th Regiment of Foot (The Royal Anglian Regiment)
The Lodge Unity No. 168 (Nova Scotia), 1771–1816

1776–77	North America,	Boston and Princetown
1778	Nova Scotia	
1799	Netherlands	
1804–23	India	

22nd (Cheshire) Regiment of Foot
The Lodge Mariah No. 132 (New York), 1767–1809

1775	North America,	Boston
1776	North America	Halifax, New York, New Jersey
1779	North America	New York City
1780	North America	Springfield, Yorktown
1793	West Indies	
1800–03	South Africa	
1803	India	Bharatpore

23rd (Royal Welch Fusiliers) Regiment of Foot
The Mason's Lodge No. 137, 1751–1816

1770–1792	North America	All battles in the American War of
		Independence
1793–94	West Indies	Saint Dominique
1799	Holland	Helder Expedition
1801	Egypt	Alexandria
1810	Spain	Peninsular War
1811–1815	Europe	Napoleonic Wars

31st (Huntingdonshire) Regiment of Foot
The St George's Lodge No. 108 (Quebec), 1761–1816

1765–74	North America	Pensacola, Florida
	North America	Saint Vincent
1776–87	Canada	Quebec
1794–97	West Indies	Martinique
	West Indies	Guadeloupe
	West Indies	St Lucia
1799–1801	Holland	
1801	Minorca	
1807	Egypt	Alexandria
1809–14	Spain	Peninsular War
1814	Sicily	

32nd (Cornwall) Regiment of Foot
White's Lodge No. 73, 1754–1809

1796	West Indies	Saint Dominique
1803	Ireland	Dublin
1807	Denmark	
1808	Portugal	

42nd (Royal Highland) Regiment of Foot
The St Andrews Lodge No. 239, 1811–1848

1809–14	Spain	Peninsular War
1815	Belgium	Battle of Waterloo

43rd (Monmouthshire) Regiment of Foot
The St Patrick's Lodge No. 156 (Quebec), 1769–1816

1774–81	North America	Lexington, Boston and Yorktown
1794–97	West Indies	Martinique
	West Indies	St Lucia
	West Indies	Guadeloupe
1807	Holland	Copenhagen
1808	Portugal	Peninsular War
1810–14	Portugal	Peninsular War
1815	North America	New Orleans
1815–18	Europe	

51st (2nd Yorkshire West Riding) Regiment of Foot
The Orange Lodge No. 213, 1806–1848

1808	Spain	Peninsular War
1815	Belgium	Battle of Waterloo

56th (West Essex) Regiment of Foot
The King George III Lodge No. 101, 1760–1809

1762–63	West Indies	Havana, Cuba
1763	Ireland	
1770–83	Gibraltar	
1788–93	Ireland	
1794–95	West Indies	Barbados
		Martinique, St Lucia and Guadeloupe
1795–98	West Indies	St Domingo

1799	Holland	Helder Expedition
1800–05	Ireland	
1805–15	India	Bom

64th (2nd Staffordshire) Regiment of Foot
The Duke of York's Lodge No. 106 (Nova Scotia), 1761–1816

1763–68	Ireland	
1768–82	North America	Boston
	North America	Halifax, Nova Scotia
	North America	Philadelphia
	North America	Charleston
1782–83	West Indies	Jamaica
1787–93	Ireland	
1793–95	West Indies	Martinique, St Lucia and Guadeloupe
1795	Gibraltar	
1798–1800	Ireland	
1800–02	West Indies	Saint Martin, St Eustatius, Saint Thomas,
	West Indies	Saint John and Saint Croix
1802–03	West indies	Barbados
	West Indies	St Lucia
1804–1814	South America	Surinam
1815-	Europe	Belgium, Battle of Waterloo

70th Regiment of Foot
The Hooker St John Lodge No. 97, 1759–1809

No movements recorded.

71st (Highland) Regiment of Foot
The Prince of Wales from Edinburgh Lodge No. 92, 1759–1809

1776–83	North America	New York, Philadelphia,
	North America	Georgia, Carolinas and Yorktown
1786–95	India	Battle of Pondicherry
1795–1802	Ceylon	
1808	Portugal/Spain	Corunna

80th (Royal Edinburgh Volunteers) Regiment of Foot
The St Andrews Lodge No. 197, 1780–1785

No postings recorded.

94th (Scots Brigade) Regiment of Foot
The Union Lodge No. 121 (USA), 1764–1809

1764–94	Holland
1796–98	South Africa
1798–1807	India
1808	Scotland

Regiment of Royal Scots Guards (2nd Dragoons)

The Royal Scots Greys Kilwinning Lodge No. 158, 1763–1770

The St Andrews Royal Arch Lodge No. 158, 1770–1816

No postings recorded.

Regiment of 3rd (Prince of Wales) Dragoon Guards
The Royal Arch Union Lodge No. 159, 1747–1816

No postings recorded.

Regiment of 7th (The Princess Royal's) Dragoon Guards 1795
The Queens Lodge No. 188, 1776–1816

No postings recorded.

Forfar and Kincardine Militia
The Lodge of Forfar & Kincardine No. 225, 1808–1815
1815 became a civilian lodge that is still current.

No Postings recorded.

2nd Argyllshire (Fencible) Regiment
The Argyllshire Military St John Lodge No. 258, 1795–1809

| 1795–1802 | Ireland |

21st (Royal North British Fusilier) Regiment of Foot
The Aboyne 6th North British Militia Lodge No. 207, 1799–

| 1814 | Holland | Bergen op Zoom |
| 1815 | North America | Battle of New Orleans |

Appendix Six
Extracts from a Talk Given by W Bro R M Lacey Entitled Masonic Heroes

Military persons known for their heroic accomplishments with masonic attachments:

2nd Lt James Wolfe 1727–1759 member of:	Marines later Brigadier Major 12th Reg. of Foot Battle of Culloden 6.4.1746 Minden Military Lodge
Arthur Wellesley 1769–1852 Duke of Wellington member of:	General in British Army Prime Minister 1828–1830 Trim Lodge No. 494 (Ireland)
James Oglethorpe 1696–1785	MP 1722. Led band of 150 people, 35 families, to the Carolinas, settling at mouth of Savannah River.
1st WM of:	Solomon's Lodge No. 1, Savannah, Georgia (USA)
Crimean War 1854–1855	Royal Artillery Regiment Florence Nightingale Lodge

	No. 706 formed specifically for victims of war.
Lt Gonville Bramhead VC	2nd Battalion 24th Regiment of Foot later South Wales Borderers
member of:	Zetland Lodge No. 515
Lt John Rouse Merriott Chard VC	Corps of Engineers Rourke's Drift, SA 1879
member of:	St George's Lodge No. 112
Lt Melvill VC member of:	Rouke's Drift, SA 1879 Leinster Lodge No. 387
Lt Melvill VC member of:	Rouke's Drift, SA 1879 Glittering Star Lodge No. 322
George Findlater VC	1st Battalion Gordon Highlanders Tirah Campaign, India 1897
member of;	Lodge St Congan No. 922
Captain Ernest Towse VC	Gordon Highlanders 2nd Boer War 1900
Field Marshall Earl Roberts VC	British Army
1832–1914	WW1
member of:	Khyber Lodge No. 582
Field Marshall Lord Kitchener	Initially Royal Engineers
1850–1916	Earl Horatio H Kitchener of Khartoum
member of:	British Union Lodge No. 114 and 14 others. Past District GM for Egypt and the Sudan
Corporal David Hunter VC 1898–1965	WW1, Moevres, France

member of:	Union Lodge No. 250
Comp Sarg't William John George Evans VC	Manchester Regiment
1876–1937	WW1, Guillemont, France
member of:	Wilton Lodge No. 1077
Sergeant Colin Fraser Barron VC	3rd Battalion 1st Central Ontario Reg
1893–1958	WW1, Battle of Passchendaele
member of:	St Andrews Lodge No. 52
Walter Brodie VC MC	Highland Light Infantry
1885–1918	WW1
member of:	Lodge Canongate Kilwinning No. 2
Lance Corporal Robert Gordon McBeath VC	Seaforth Highlanders
1897–1922	WW1, Cambrai, France
member of:	St Mary's Caledonian Operative Lodge No. 339
Cyril Royston Bassett VC	New Zealand Expeditionary Force WW1 Gallipoli, Italy
member of:	Ara Lodge No. 1 Auckland, NZ
Lt Sir Tasker Watkins VC	WW1, Normandy, France
member of:	
Sgt Major Charles Coward	Awarded Iron Cross
1905–1979	WW2
member of:	Camberwell Old Comrades Lodge No. 4077

Appendix Seven
Research Material

1. 'How Scotland's independence was lost'
The Week 5 July 2014
2. *'The Temple and the Lodge'*
by Michael Baigent and Richard Leigh
Published by Jonathan Cape 1987
3. *'The Freemasons' Guide and Compendium'* by Bernard E Jones
Published by Harrap 1950
4. *'The Oxford Illustrated History of Britain'* by Kenneth O Morgan
Published by Oxford University Press 1984
5. *'William Pitt the Younger'* by William Hague
Published by Harper Collins 2004
6. *'Scottish Golf History'* from their website
7. *'Golf in Montrose'* by William Coull 1993
Published by Montrose Links
8. Club History of Fraserburgh Golf Club from their website
9. Club History of Burntisland Golf Club from their website

10. Club History of Cruden Bay Golf Club from the Scottish History website
11. Club History of Fortrose and Rosemarkie Golf Club from their website
12. Club History of Dunbar Golf Club from their website
13. *'The History of Golf in Northern Scotland c. 1600–1800'* by Dr Wade Cormack *Through the Green,* September 2018
14. '*Early Golf in England (1606–1659)*' by Neil S Miller—*Through the Green*, September 2016
15. '*Leith to Muirfield via Musselburgh*' by Bobby Burt—*Through the Green*, September 2013
16. *'Golf—History and Tradition 1500–1945'*—Chapter Three.

'The Formation of Golf Clubs' by David Stirk

Published by Excellent Press 1998

17. *'Golf—the History of an Obsession'* by David Stirk

Published by Phaidon Press 1995

18. *'Chronicles of Golf 1457–1857', 'Golf and the Freemasons' 1766–1775* by Alistair J Johnston and James F Johnston

Published by International Merchandising Corporation 1993

19. *'Royal Blackheath'* by Ian T Henderson and David Stirk

Published by Henderson and Stirk 1981

20. Notes on the 22 Gentlemen who purchased the silver club of the Society of Golfers at St Andrews 1754 from *'Golf—History and Tradition'* by David Stirk
21. Notes on the R & A Golf Club by Angela Howe—Director of Museum & Heritage

22. *'The Bruntsfield Links Golfing Society 1761–2011'* by Pat Colledge

Published by St Andrews Golf Press 2012

23. Further notes on Bruntsfield Links Golfing Society from Pat Colledge
24. *'Anent the Golf—'* concerning Glasgow Golf Club by Nevin McGhee, *Through the Green*, September 2012
25. Further notes on Glasgow Golf Club from Nevin McGhee
26. Notes on Old Manchester (Club) from Graham Waters
27. Notes on the Leven Golf Clubs from Archie Shanks
28. History of Prestwick Golf Club from their website
29. Notes on Portobello Golf Club from Czeslaw Kruk
30. *'Dunbar Golf'* by J V Harris

Published by J V Harris 2007

31. *'400 Years of the Blackheath Golfer'* by Neil Scaife

Published by Royal Blackheath GC 2009

32. *'The XVIIIth Century in London'* by E Beresford Chancellor

Published by B T Batsford Ltd 1920

33. *'Golf—Scotland's Game'* A Hidden Club by David Hamilton

Published by Partick Press Ltd 1998

34. *'Lodge of Good Report No. 136 and its Meeting Places'* A Further History by H R Sharp
35. *'Scottish Golf History'* The Role of Early Speculative Freemasons by Neil Laird

Published by the website of Scottish Golf History

36. *'History of British and Colonial Regiments and their Military Lodges' Wikipedia*

37. *'When Dressing for Golf Required Uniformity'*
by Bobby Burt, *Through the Green*, June 2014
38. Notes on *'The 1799 Unlawful Societies Act'* from John Harris
39. Details of *'The Unlawful Societies Act of 1799'* from Wikipedia
40. *'History of the Camden Place Lodge'* by John Attenborough and William Mitchell

Published by Chislehurst GC in booklet form.

41. *'100 Years of Golf at Camden Place'* History of Chislehurst Golf Club by W M Mitchell

Published by Grant Books 1994

42. *'The Rosslyn Hoax?'* by Robert L D Cooper

Published by Lewis Masonic 2006

43. *'The Genesis of Freemasonry'* by David Harrison

Published by Lewis Masonic 2009

44. *'Working as One'* by John Hamill—*Freemasonry Today Dec 2013*

45. *'The Origins of Freemasonry'* by David Stevenson

Published by Cambridge University Press 1988

46. *'Early Masonic Catechisms'* by Harry Carr

Published by Quatuor Coronati Lodge No. 2076, 1975

47. History of Lanark Golf Club—military connections from their website
48. *'The First Golf Club in Ireland'*

Col. William H Gibson, *Through the Green*, September 2012 and December 2012

49. *'The London Scottish Golf Club'* by John Downs

Published by the London Scottish Golf Club 2004

50. Notes on the formation of the Wimbledon Golf Clubs from Hugh Grieve

51. '*Delving Further Beyond the Craft*' by Rev'd Neville Barker Cryer

Published by Lewis Masonic 2009

52. The History of The Savannah Golf Club from their website

53. '*Golf in New York 1779–1785*' by Col. William H Gibson, *Through the Green*, March 2015

54. *'Evidence of Golf in Gibraltar'* by Neil Millar, William Gibson and David Hamilton, *Through the Green*, June 2013

55. '*Golf in South Africa*' by Lieutenant-General Sir Robert Richardson, *Through the Green*, December 2013

56. '*The Multifaceted Mason*' by Dr James Campbell, *Freemasonry Today*, Winter 2018

57. *'A Short History of the Armed Forces and Masonry'* by VWBro Brig. P R Sharpe PGSwdB, The Circuit of Service Lodges—militarymasons.org.uk

58. *'Military Golfers in the Waterloo Campaign'* by Col. William H Gibson, *Through the Green*, June 2015

59. *British & Colonial Regiments and their Military Lodges*—Vol. 1 Parts 1 and 2 *Wikipedia*

60. *Masonic Heroes*—extracts from a talk given by W Bro R M Lacey *LGRA Bulletin No. 216*

61. '*I Just Didn't Know That*' by Rev'd Neville Barker Cryer

Published by Lewis Masonic 2013

62. *'The Oldest Club in the Southern Hemisphere'* the Mauritius Golf Club by Bob Fletcher & Richard Williams *Through the Green,* Sept 2019

63. *'Early Golf in Mauritius'* The Mauritius Military Gymkhana Club by Bob Fletcher & Richard Williams *Through the Green,* March 2020
64. *'Golf—The Early Days (1995)'* by Dale Concannon Published by Salamander Books, 1995
65. '*Military Golfers in the Jacobite Rising 1745–1746'* By Col. William H Gibson, *Through the Green* December 2021
66. *'Consequences of the 1723 Constitutions part 2: France'* By Dr Ric Berman, *Freemasonry Today*, Summer 2023.
67. *'The Polite Revolution: The formation of American Grand Lodges 1777–1806'* By S Brent Morris. *Quatuor Coronati,* Vol 116, 2003.
68. *'The Great English Golf Boom: A History 1964–1914' Written and published by Michael B Morrison. 2022*
69. *The Craft: How the freemasons made the modern world, by John Dickie. Published by Hodder & Stoughton 2020*